The Heart of the Serpent

The Heart of the Serpent

Mystical Journeys to the Core of Life

Luis De La Lama

THE HEART OF THE SERPENT.
Copyright © 1993
by Luis De La Lama.
All rights reserved.
Printed in the United States of
America. No part of this book may be
used or reproduced in any manner
whatsoever without written permission
except in case of brief quotations
embodied in critical articles and
reviews. For information address
White Dragon Productions
P.O. Box 68124,
Raleigh, NC 27613
or
STAR*LIFE
1295 South Kihei Rd., Suite 3009
Kihei, Maui, HI 96753

ISBN: 1-883381-42-8
LCCN: 93-60379

To my mother, who gave me love.
To my father, who gave me freedom.
To Luisa, my Twin Soul, who inspired me.
To Life at Large.

ACKNOWLEDGMENTS

Many have given me the seeds of thought and experience that are the basis for this book; they did this by word, deed, or omission.

Some contributed by their mere company, inadvertently. Some initiated and instructed me in the secret lodges of diverse esoteric associations. I won't mention their titles or functions because what I acknowledge here is their unpretentious generosity.

My appreciation to Domingo Díaz Porta, Refugio Padilla, Celia Pallares, Jesús Aguirre, Octavio Nahum, Héctor Seemann, Walter Rudametkin, Hermenegildo Rivas, Fran Keegan, Dolores Ashckroft-Nowicky, Hariharananda, Corey Vian, Gyaltrul Rimpoche, Dada Sumatrananda, and especially A—, my teacher of hermeticism and magic.

My gratitude to my students, past and present. Their faith and curiosity has always prompted me to reach higher.

My thanks to Myra Parisoff, Ph. D., the editor of this book. Her expertise in English literature as well as metaphysics and abstract thinking came to me as a gift from heaven.

INTRODUCTION

*E*verything I write about in my book is genuine, although my interpretation of these events and visions is based on esoteric modalities of thought.

This book came to be because it had to. It embodies the convergence of personal and transpersonal forces: The petty search for recognition and the fraternal ideal of sharing my awareness align with the currents of life that use my personality as an interface between the noumenal and phenomenal worlds.

At first, this book's magical universe appears to be an intoxicating array of random self-active psychic materials that coalesce in the attic of my mind and scatter my life in unexpected directions. Behind this seemingly entropic landscape there is a powerful subjacent force field: that of the Magus, the archetypal being who in the process of manipulating the forces of life becomes one with them.

If you look for a cosmology in these pages you will waste your time. I don't offer a theoretical model to classify my perceptions because it would limit the ways my writing fertilizes your consciousness.

However, entering a magical universe is like walking through kaleidoscopic realms; it is easy to get lost in the ever-changing mystical landscapes. To integrate the wealth of information that assails perception in the process of enlightenment, I used many paradigms. I offer the simplest here.

In this paradigm three main levels are involved in expanding awareness: the level of the ordinary self or the personality; the soul, sharing transpersonal levels of consciousness with archetypal forces that regulate evolution of mankind and nature; and the spirit, or what might be called the real self, as source, nourishment, and essence of everything on all levels of existence.

The spirit is that immanent, eternal, self sustained oneness that you might have read about in many of the holy books. The soul is for me a field of energy and consciousness responsive to mysterious archetypal rhythms. The personality perceives these fluctuations through the slot of linear time and interprets them as changes in one's physical and psychological life.

The archetypal forces reorganize themselves continuously in diverse configurations, like pieces of glass in an infinite kaleidoscope. From the level of the spirit these reconfigurations are irrelevant to the essence of the kaleidoscope. The personality, however, is always dazzled by the ever-changing patterns perceived as the richness of sensorial, emotional, and mental experience.

Perception at soul level intuits order in the cosmic scheme; sometimes, however, you might be temporarily seduced by the transpersonal forces and identify with the predominant colors in the kaleidoscopic view.

When consciousness sees from the spirit, all is One; change is an illusion in the circus of time. This state of consciousness is beyond language or logic; the wise ones of old used paradox to refer to it, for example, "the squaring of the circle," meaning that the spirit (circle) is one with manifestation (the square).

The path to higher awareness is not linear; it rather resembles a tango dance, consciousness moves forward and backward. While many spiritual teachers consider inability to fix consciousness at the highest point a human weakness, I believe this happens for a reason: the ultimate goal of human evolution is *not* to achieve permanent residence in the lofty spiritual world, but to glide through the different levels at will. True human development is for me the freedom to focus between all-inclusiveness and individuality.

Beyond this rough sketch of what happens to the evolving consciousness, I developed a system to face new experiences. Throughout the book's chapters my routes are addressed from different angles to bring to light the details of each strategy, as well as their interlinking, into a coherent system. My ways involve:

- Self-honesty and boldness that lead to new forms of perception.
- Originality and resolution, despite faddish collective trends.
- Acceptance of the entire spectrum of human sensations and emotions; in essence, all the cosmic forces encountered on the inner path of the spirit.
- Integration of power through alignment with the mighty archetypal vectors that shape our innermost drives and life as we experience it.
- Living in the understanding that one's sense of personal identity changes all the time. Considering the "me" as a paradoxical epiphenomenon in the dimensions of higher awareness.

Every chapter is a cluster of psychic meaning; I disclose constellations of related events the way memories are stored. My writing is not meant to satisfy reason, but to enkindle the soul.

I don't want to make sense, but to nourish and inflame with essence.

I want you to know that there are dimensions of being that are richer, more sophisticated, and more fulfilling than anything you have experienced before. I want you to know that to enter one of these dimensions of being you need to be attentive and honest about your real nature, as well as courageous, focused, and persevering to unfold it into an enjoyable reality. I want you to know that from one of those majestic dimensions of being your genius has the power to set the standards around you.

This book is, as anything else in the universe, an echo of the original sound of creation that wells from your true essence, a sound that is always returning to you, from many directions, reminding you of its source.

Luis De La Lama

CONTENTS

Introduction		*ix*
1	Journey to the Land of the Shamans	*3*
2	Magic Mushrooms on the Sacred Mountain	*21*
3	Carlos Castaneda and the Warrior's Eagle	*33*
4	Climbing Out of the Abyss	*49*
5	The Paths That Made My Path	*67*
6	My Experience of the Goddess	*85*
7	The Discovery of My Mission	*107*
8	Business As Usual	*121*
9	Navigating Through Fear	*147*
10	Outer Darkness and the Moving Center of Light	*169*
Epilogue		*189*
Index		*191*

The Heart of the Serpent

1

JOURNEY TO THE LAND OF THE SHAMANS

Meeting face to face with the archaic forces of nature in the mystic Mixtec land of central México is like a little death. It is like a little death because, among other things, even before the confrontation, spontaneously you review your whole life. I was flying to Oaxaca, México, when an inner urge compelled me to write on loose sheets of paper the following:

> "My mother told me that when I was a few days old she took me to the church, and in front of an image of Jesus Christ she prayed with all her heart for me to be different from anybody else she knew. She prayed to Jesus Christ for me to be like him.

Somehow, this deep magical act from a soul that my far memory recognized as a priestess of Isis imprinted me for life. This consecration to our culture's highest model has been both a blessing and a heavy burden on me. It hasn't been easy trying to be like Jesus Christ, but I do not regret this noble event in 1956 at one of the little churches in Tijuana, México. I know it happened for a reason, a reason that stands clear to me now after years and years of traveling among the transpersonal levels of consciousness.

My life now is the best I have ever had. I have many reasons to feel proud of it. I am the founder of a system for spiritual enlightenment not based on indoctrination of any kind. I have activated cosmic energies in students in Europe, Asia, and America. My job is to do magic every day. In a matter of minutes I can transform forever the energy fields of my students. I bring diverse, infinite, undepletable energies and change my students' auras in a way that allows them to receive and reproduce at any time and any place that same power. My students use these energies for a wide range of applications: cleansing of disturbed thoughts and emotions, acceleration of physical healing, and spiritual growth, among others.

I am respected, loved, and admired by many, but my private life is even more fulfilling. I am married to a goddess incarnate in every sense of the word. We have been together for three years and our love and fusion keeps growing every day. Her children, that I love like my own, are smart, uninhibited, and attractive. Our financial situation is going well, and the only thing I could ask from life now is more time to spend with my family.

Is that true? No! I am writing this on a plane that is taking me to adventure and risk. I have a flame inside that never dies. It consumes me with greed for achievement, although the achievement I look for is not of this world.

I have practiced ritual magic since I was seventeen. I have invoked angels and demons, gods and goddesses, masters of wisdom, and have received answers. My life has been full of truthful and accurate telepathic messages. My spiritual eye is open to a good degree and, although from a higher, mystical perspective, I know all those beings are all part of my All-containing universal Self. Yet I still enjoy communicating with these beings, which, nevertheless, from a magical perspective, are real on their own level of existence.

This inner flame of passion for the beyond, this unquenchable thirst for oneness, this obsession of my spirit for marriage with all that is subtle and extraordinary is dragging me to the Mexican sierra where I am going to bet my physical health and my sanity for the reward of a higher level of enlightenment.

It is true that I am a seasoned traveler in the realms of higher consciousness. I have felt one with Infinity many times. Over many years of discipline in yoga and meditation I have a fair amount of control over my mind, and I have done enough research on hallucinogenics to feel confident of success.

The point of all this is: Why can't I relax in the achievements of the present? Why is change always calling me with the luring voice of a mermaid? Why am I not able to resist its charms? Why this eternal longing? Sometimes, as I spend my days traveling to confer the Cosmic Activations of my energy system, I think I am like Hermes, the patron of the Hermetic mysteries, the winged god of the magicians. Too much of him in me perhaps? Yes, I am happy with my life, but I wonder if I will ever be satisfied.

This fire has been burning inside me as long as I can remember. I spent my first sixteen years in restless and uncoordinated daydreaming. The urge for the supernatural took me to the study of Greek mythology, as well as to astrology and yoga. I was born with the feeling that I had a mission, something to do that would benefit humanity. I always wanted to help people, although my emotional nature was not mature enough to find an effective way. Feeling different made me introverted; nobody could understand something I was still unable to put into words.

In awe of that transcendental Self I intuited from an early age that everything else was a shadow. It has taken my whole life to see this transcendental Self throbbing in the physical world around me, yet it still escapes when I look for it. I chase the transcendental Self through the labyrinths of life, like the great Universal Serpent that bites its own tail. I discovered a long time ago that my personality was like the tail of the serpent. Sometimes I'm brave and courageously penetrate deeper into its entrails, looking for its heart. Sometimes I'm afraid and stop; then I see the Serpent of Life devouring me deeper into its body. I seldom recognize that the Serpent and I are One."

The airport in México City is busier than eighteen years ago when I used it to travel back and forth to Tijuana, my native city. I feel strange now. I realize I'm a citizen of two worlds, and, in truth, I belong to neither one of them.

The city is enjoying a clear day. These don't come too often, although today the winds are benevolent so that from the plane I can see its two famous volcanoes as well as the second most-populated city in the world fully laid out before me.

After crossing the mountains that separate the Mexican capital from Oaxaca, my energy changes; I feel my heart opening in expectation. I have never been in Oaxaca before, but my sense of connection with the land becomes evident even before the landing. I am lucky. This is the time of year when the whole valley is green and everything looks beautiful.

After picking up my bags I wait for ten minutes at the airport. I know Mexicans do not concern themselves with time, so I relax according to the custom of the country. After awhile I see a young man shyly holding a gray piece of cardboard with my name written in green.

Promptly I am taken to the Marques del Valle Hotel in the central plaza of Oaxaca, an austere building with colonial architecture. I can't say the room is cozy, but who needs coziness when the temperature is 82°F? Later I would be glad I did not forget my earplugs, since my room had a view to the plaza and the traffic was loud until late at night. When I open the water faucet I can clearly see a brownish liquid carrying Montezuma's revenge. There's nothing to fear; the hotel has bottled water on each floor. Besides, I came prepared with disinfectant pills.

My guides are a couple of professors who happen to be distant relatives of a man whom I knew from a meditation circle in northern México six years ago. He told me about a fascinating experience he had with a shaman in the mountains toward the coast—and I have come all the way from North Carolina to see this individual. My guides have other plans, too; they want me to see as many healers as they know. Perhaps in this way I will not be so disappointed if we cannot find the magic-mushroom shaman at all. They don't lose any time and bring me to the first healer right away.

Angela Rios is a famous miracle healer who is no longer active. She is a woman of about fifty years, tall and slender for her age and race, with an aura of integrity that forces you to love her. She lives in San Felipe del Agua and takes care of a tiny market store. First she studies us with a deep look, then she invites us to sit below a vine in her backyard.

In a sad voice she tells about the group-sorcery attack she underwent seven years ago when the evil energy cast by jealous competitive healers over her temple and herself created a serious accident that "disconnected her brain" and prevented any subsequent healing work.

Between sights she explains the differences between energy work that impresses so many people these days and the real spiritual healing she used to do. True spiritual healing stays, she says, miracles are forever, and they only happen with the intervention of God. After awhile Angela seems to feel comfortable with us.

With her eyes fixed in the distance, her voice drops a little, and, as if to herself, she describes the good old days: "I used to have hundreds coming from all over México and other countries. My spiritual servant [as she refers to the spiritual servant of God, the spiritual entity that healed through her body] often healed people who had been cast out of hospitals to die. He gave them herbs, but the herbs were merely the vehicles for his power and the power of God.

"There was a girl who couldn't be healed by doctors. Her parents belonged to an evangelical group that prayed several days for her without results. The parents didn't ask for my help because they knew they would be criticized by others in the church, but they had been my friends in the past and I knew and liked the girl. So I went to visit the family and waited until the prayer circle had left. Then I went out of my body. When I returned the girl's parents told me my spiritual servant, talking through my mouth, had informed them that it was nothing serious. It was only a bad spirit who had taken possession of the body of the innocent creature. My spiritual servant told them he had expelled the bad spirit and the girl would be in a perfect state of health the next day. As he said it happened.

Later, when other spiritualistic groups began losing their congregations to join mine, some of the *materias* [or women who channel the healing spirits] became jealous of my work and swore they would stop me. The energy in my temple became fouled for years. My husband and I did many *limpias* [or spiritual purifications], but my power was so weak after the sorcery attack that we couldn't keep our spiritual work. It's been a long time now, but my spiritual servant has recently told me I will be called to do healing work and will have a big congregation again. Then I will confer *catedras* [or teachings from the spiritual entity directed to the congregation through the voice of the medium]."

As a woman approaches Angela's house, she stops a few yards from us in a shy and respectful way, never looking up from the ground. Angela excuses herself momentarily and talks with the woman. They lower their voices and their expressions are serious. By the look in her eyes you can tell the woman needs help. I can pick up a few words—red candles...Friday night... Angela is teaching a sorcery technique to the woman. I'm curious but do not inquire; that would have been disrespectful.

When the woman departs, Angela returns to us and gives us an update of what is happening in the spiritual communities in rural México: "Now there are several new religions coming from the U.S.A.; they lure people into their churches by impressing them with their big expensive temples. They lend them money and offer them jobs. When they prosper enough they come to their houses to register all they have. If they have two chickens, they take one for the church. If they have only one, they forbid them to eat it without paying half of the chicken's value to the church. Many people want to leave those churches today, but they can't because they owe most of what they have to them. The worst part of all of this is that all their prayers are ineffective; they are unable to heal."

I offer my humble energy work to help her "connect with her brain" again. She takes me into her sanctum and I can feel that the energy is pure now. Everything is white inside, with a seven-step dais with oil lamps on each step, and images of Christ, the Virgin, and a painting of the symbolic eye in the triangle shedding light onto the world. I work for five minutes on her and she looks happier, younger, thankful. She invites me the next day to visit an active healer who is almost as good as she was.

Unfortunately, I have plans for tomorrow. I hug her with sincere affection, then wishing her a fast "brain reconnection," we depart.

On my first night in Oaxaca I dream that I'm lying flat on the ground below the foliage of an immense tree. A huge dark python is descending from a tree branch directly over my body. The snake has two heads, but I manage to catch them with a firm grip before the rest of the serpent touches me. Although its scales are rough and its body bumpy, I feel an archaic beingness that coexists with my perception of the danger I am in. As the serpent keeps moving down across my body, I feel its massive weight. It is burying me below its body, but I get no sense of evil, no intention to harm me from its behavior. I only sense an inevitability. One part of me is fully alert; the other feels confident of the outcome. This part feels certain I will be able to control the serpent's two jaws and the movements of its body.

Upon awakening I realize that my dream is very auspicious; it contains the archetypal Tree of Life and the Serpent of Wisdom. I know that universal currents are coming my way.

We had made plans to leave at 3 pm for the secret place where the magic-mushroom shaman lives. My guides had been there six years ago and feel very confident in locating the healer's house. We finally get out of Oaxaca at 5:48. A mechanical checkup for the truck and haggling over buying a thick plastic tarp to cover the passengers in the back prevents us from departing on time.

As we travel for several hours on a road that often has the texture of a moon landscape, I discover the members of my group are not really certain of our destination. In the beginning they think it is before Miahuatlán; then that it should be before San José del Pacífico, then before San José del Alto, and we keep running through all the little towns one after another. As it gets dark, my travel guides start asking directions. Those outside the truck take a long time to answer. They look as if they are digging in the depths of time to rescue a memory. Finally, they come out of their trance with a triumphal set of instructions that later proves to be either a lie or a gross miscalculation. This pattern is repeated three times along the road to the coast. There are no road signs for many of the villages, and our little map by the Secretaría de Turismo does not mention at all the place for which we are looking. When we stop at San José del Pacífico at 10 pm, I buy apples from a man with keen unblinking eyes and a perpetually mischievous smile. I remember thinking that this man looked just as I imagined Don Juan when I first read the Carlos Castaneda books. I ask him if he knows who sells mushrooms in the area. He says that everybody is asleep now, but he might have information for us the next day. Then I join with my guides who are having chocolate and sweet bread at the village *fonda* [or little café]. One of the guides asks where we can get some mushrooms. Those who are supposed to answer react in a strange way; they say no in the shortest and faintest way possible. They never look at us again as their energy seems to vanish in a misty fog. Their bodies look like cardboard, and you simply know in your soul it is impossible to ask them another question.

It is 11 pm when one of my guides (and I hesitate to call them guides anymore) seems to recognize some natural landmarks. The way the road turns and a stream that crosses below are enough to cause a reaction to burst from his almost-frozen brain. It's cold up there in the mountains, and we, as good Mexicans, did not come prepared for it. The old truck's heater no longer works, and the coats and blankets in it are not enough for all of us.

We stand out below an imposing sky that mercilessly showers the brilliance of its stars on the gates of our awareness. It's difficult to think of anything else; even the cold seems to be eclipsed by the majesty of the high Mexican sierra. We have electric handlights that allow us to explore a few yards beyond the paved road, but we find no traces of civilization.

Prompted by the aesthetic power that nature exerts over me, I expand my awareness and try to enter the shaman's wavelength; I do not get an answer and feel discouraged. Was it a silly idea to travel all the way down to this place in the hope of finding a mysterious man who was seen for the last time about nine years before? Perhaps I should accept the fact that those three days in Oaxaca would be spent visiting museums, ruins, folk art, and enduring the dull tour to the temples of the urban healers. After all, perhaps the magic-mushroom experience is not for me, only for those who are not as refined and as gifted as this wonderful man in my shoes.

Suddenly I hear the laughter of children in my brain. As we are walking back to the truck, I have to keep an eye out for obstacles on the ground. But this is no inconvenience to the voices that, like a choir of smart and playful children, are singing a short message to me: "We love you. You'll be with us soon. You'll find us. It'll be okay." Soon after hearing the voices I recover my good spirits.

We drive another ten kilometers toward the coast. There are no more signs of human life and the cold is getting worse. We see an isolated house on the left side of the road and head toward it to ask for directions. It is our last hope that night.

The dogs are barking furiously and we do not dare come close. We yell to the people inside for about three minutes without an answer, repeating over and over: "Good night! We are lost! We need directions! We are looking for Don Constantino. Do you know where he lives?"

We are beginning to think there is nobody inside, but we insist once more: "We just crossed a stream. Does he live to the right of the road?"

"Yes!" answers a child, its voice barely audible from between the dried branches stuck together with metallic wire and dried mud that constitute the house walls. There is no light inside. It takes ten more minutes to get a few more words from the child and the scared woman inside. They have to repeat their instructions many times to compete with the barking of the dogs and the sound of the old truck's motor, still running since the owner fears the battery might die.

We drive back to the place where the stream crosses the road. Don Constantino and his family live deeper in the sierra. It's just a matter of a short walk and crossing a ten-foot-wide stream over a flexible piece of wood that emphasizes the uncertainty of our steps with undulations that make our walk more difficult as we advance. It feels as if the spirit of the narrow wood below our feet avenges its low position with this malevolent game that spirals up in a vicious circle of almost catastrophic consequences as we try to reach the other side. Next morning we will discover that what looked like a rushing, dangerous current is only a few inches deep.

It is past midnight when we find ourselves yelling again, this time in front of three little houses located uphill. The houses do not have electricity, but we see in the starlit night two figures emerging from one of the houses. After we identify ourselves and state our purpose, they let us come in.

The man lights an ocote splinter, a resinous wood that is equivalent to a single candle light, but it is not bright enough to get a reliable impression of him. The first thing I notice about Don Constantino is his untidiness. His coat is greasy, dirty, and worn out. His fingernails are long and the dirt beneath them makes the tips look black. The whole place is filthy and smells like chicken dung.

To alleviate my disappointment I think of the stories of Tibetan masters who present themselves in the most-repulsive disguises to test disciples in search of enlightenment. I try hard not to judge this man, but in the bottom of my heart I would have wished my guru to be as clean as the Pope and as exotic as a Rock Star.

He explains to us that mushrooms are very difficult to find now, the rain has not been plentiful, and he has collected none this year. We persuade him to extend his hospitality to us for the night and to take us mushroom hunting next morning. Before retiring to bed he tells us the story of his first encounter with the world of the magical mushrooms.

Twenty years ago he was living in the woods and had severe problems with his wife. One day he noticed one of those mushrooms his grandfathers had shown him many years before. He remembered his words: "When a magic mushroom crosses your way, you must eat it or something bad will happen to you. You might get a poisonous snake bite or experience some other calamity."

Upon eating the mushroom, he heard its voice telling him clearly and precisely where his problem originated: his father had been attacked by means of sorcery used to drive him from a valuable piece of land. However, the one who received the negative energy blow was Constantino because he used to drink and was not as strong etherically as his father. The mushroom gave him a ritualistic procedure to reflect the curse, and recommended he should tell the perpetrators of the crime that he knew they had used evil arts. Now they should ask forgiveness from Don Constantino's father or the bouncing back of the curse would kill their own son in three days.

He did not tell anybody this because he didn't want to be known as a sorcerer himself, but acted on the other recommendations of the mushroom. Three days later the eight-year-old son of the antagonist was dead. After that event he stopped drinking and began his learning from the mushrooms. He then gave us a taste of what to expect from a magic-mushroom trip: "When there is only one mushroom in the field and you eat it, its voice is most clear and pure. If you find them in bunches, their messages are more difficult to understand.

"When the mushrooms appear during midsummer days, the visions they bring are lower in nature. You see dragons and serpents. The mushrooms from September are those which bring the highest visions, those of Jesus Christ, the Virgin, the Divine Child, angels, and the old wise ones with long white beards."

He speaks about three different species of hallucinogenic mushrooms: "The black mushrooms are not as good. The *pajaritos* [little birds] are regular, but the white ones are the best. They can teach many different things. Sometimes the people I help, eat them with me, but sometimes I am the one who eats them and gives them information about their problems. Sometimes the mushrooms heal them right on the spot, such as the time a man saw how they were dismembering his whole body, then put him back in one piece. The back pain that made him walk crooked disappeared forever and he regained his normal posture."

We spend the night in the filthiest place I have ever been, cold as hell, waking up thirty times a night with a cramp or a numb limb. We try to sleep on *petates,* a kind of mat one-fourth of an inch thick, but only the width and size of the human body, made by intercrossing fibrous dried leaves like those from palm trees. These primitive mats were placed over a damp, cement floor, the room temperature at 35°F. The cold wind circulated through the innumerable openings between the boards that constituted the walls. Sometimes the wind came from the W.C. At those times you'd rather have slept outside or spent all night out in the dark doing aerobics. Noises of mice and other animals were heard all night. We had to get rid of the cockroaches that crawled on our *petates* at times. It was bad, but we survived.

Don Constantino mentioned the night before that we should be ready for the mushroom hunt at seven in the morning. He was speaking Mexican time, which for non-Latin countries meant about 9:30. I did not regret this delay at all; we had an excellent breakfast of what the civilized world would have called organic coffee, organic tortillas, and organic eggs—all prepared by Margarita, Don Constantino's wife. She also cooked every day for the construction workers Don Constantino hired to build a new house. We all sat in a very small room darkened with smoke from the wood used in the kitchen. Our eyes were full of tears from the clouds of smoke and the chili sauce.

The breakfast was especially good because Don Constantino tastefully spiced it with more stories of sorcery: "Years ago when I worked cutting wood, they hired us in groups and we lived together for several months. There was a man who never ate with us; he used to take his food to a remote spot where he was sometimes heard growling like a cat. It wasn't until later when we discovered the loss of a goat, chickens, and a pig that we realized the strange man was a *nagual* [in this context, a shape-shifter]. The other workers promptly killed him since they couldn't afford the loss of more valuable animals. Of course, the animals stopped disappearing once the man who transformed into an animal had been executed. . .

"During a mushroom trip, you can go to a place where you see a queen with a beautiful crystal wheel of fortune. The wheel of fortune has children inside who are the souls of dead infants. Black sorcerers, who are hired to cause suffering to others, pray to this Queen of the Wheel of Fortune to take the souls of the children of the enemies of their clients. . .

"Once during a mushroom session I saw the Evil King. He wore a crooked metal mask and had crooked arms, torso, and legs. The Evil King wanted to kill me. I demanded an explanation of his behavior. He said he had been sent by a sorcerer hired by a family who hated my intervention in state politics. I demonstrated to the Evil King my intentions were good and I had no reason to die. After a long time I won the Evil King to my side and this monstrous psychic entity told me how to reflect the spell on those who sent him. They all died within the next three years. Unfortunately, others who have seen the Evil King in their visions are only allowed to know about their terrible fate, but not given a way to escape it...

"There are some spots on the sierra where crying children, big bulls, dogs, and other phantasmagoric figures appear. These beings chase the peasants. Often those who see them get sick with *susto* [fear], and after their strength abandons them they die. If these poor people are correctly diagnosed, and if they follow the prescribed remedies, they can be cured. The healing procedures include things such as bathing in springs for a certain number of days or cleansing the energy field with an egg to absorb the negative energy. After this kind of cleansing treatment, the egg is cracked and inside the shell there should appear something resembling blood, organic fibers, an animal such as a frog, a worm, or even a serpent."

During the daylight it is easier to appreciate Don Constantino's presence. There is something about him that makes us feel confident. Perhaps it is because he is humble and unpretentious. You know he will never take advantage of you. When he tells his horror stories they are a matter of fact for him. He is not trying to impress you at all.

Not all of the stories are macabre. Don Constantino also told us about some of the many fantastic healings he has done with the help of the magic mushrooms. They tell him which plants to use to cure those who come to visit him. Don Constantino's children have never seen a doctor. He has four daughters ranging in age from four to twelve. Judging by the filth I see all around, this should be one of his greatest miracles as a healer.

One of his healing formulas reveals the bizarre tapestry of religious thought: "There is a Madonna of the Mixtec lands, Our Lady of Santa Lucia. This Virgin is called only on December 13. You can pray to her in the morning to experience the miraculous removal of eye cataracts, or in the evening around 9 pm if you want the miraculous removal of a neighbor from the land around yours."

After breakfast, lead by Don Constantino, we went to look for the mushrooms. He has told us he is 56, but he looks as if he is 35, and climbs uphill as if he were 20. We follow him, panting behind. We take a 45° steep path on the slippery terrain of the Oaxaca sierra. We walk at a killing pace for thirty minutes. Way above the mountains we look for the magic mushrooms for an hour, but they elude us. We find at least twenty other species, but none of them is magical. I try to use my E.S.P. to locate the species we are looking for but to no avail. I start to doubt the truth of those little voices of last night. At this point I didn't know it was all a matter of time.

Don Constantino says that there has not been enough rain. Exhausted and disillusioned we come down slowly while he shares more of the magic-mushroom world: "Once the mushrooms told me they would stop appearing at a certain spot where I used to collect them, but would appear later on another side of the mountain. Thanks to their information, I found the new ones without any problem.

It is okay to give away the mushrooms or to receive donations, and there is no problem if the second owner sells them. Those who pick the mushrooms should not sell them at all. If they do so, the mushrooms will kill them or their families. Several of my friends have died when the little mushrooms punish their greed."

When we return to the house Don Constantino gives me several dried mushrooms. He doesn't seem too interested in leading me that evening on a mushroom journey with these old, weak mushrooms; besides, I'm not too eager to eat those moldy black pieces we all have handled with dirty hands. He indicates to me the recommended dosage. He never charges for his work, but following the tradition, I honor his time and wisdom with my own crystallized energy, money, and after a short farewell, my friends and I depart. On our return we again pass through San José del Pacífico. Since it is a clear day I can appreciate even more the beauty of this little mountain village that looks out onto a landscape prettier than the best Austrian postcards. Its beauty, its earthy energy, its virginal growth, and its potential magic that grows even more lush during the rainy season makes it the most wonderful place I have ever been.

This time I go alone and ask the man with the apples if he can help me find what we are looking for. He goes and talks to the same group of people who refused to answer my friend's question last night. They look at us for awhile. The whole time I'm broadcasting telepathically: "Yes, we will not harm you! We are nice people!" It works! A woman makes an almost inconspicuous signal to us, so we follow her. Soon we are introduced to a few specimens of *Psylocybe cubensis* and *Psylocybe caerulescens zapotecorum*. The mushrooms are carefully buried in humid soil in a deep kitchen dish. "They were found three days ago," the woman says; "These are the white ones, the *derrumbes* [overturns]." She tells me I will need about ten small ones for a full trip, and I weigh her recommendation with my previous readings... Yes, ten little mushrooms averages fifty grams. She seems to know what she is talking about. I choose twelve little mushrooms that seem to smile at me from between my hands as I pick them up.

The woman seems a little bit nervous. I ask her if she is having problems with the army or the police. She says that she has always been safe, but the people who bought mushrooms from her in past years were severely abused by the police. They were robbed of all they had and were beaten unconscious. She assures me that since the mushroom fad is in serious decline now, the Mexican army and gangs of policemen do not show up that often anymore. I note the vibrations in the air. There is good energy around. I know nothing bad will happen before we get out of San José del Pacífico, and I am enthusiastic to experience tomorrow.

On the trip back home I learn that wasp larvae, certain ants, and a particular kind of worm are considered tasty seasonal dishes when prepared correctly by means of authentic regional cooking.

2
MAGIC MUSHROOMS ON THE SACRED MOUNTAIN

The evening of our return from the mountains I prepare myself for the next day's events. I spend most of my time in meditation and only go out for a short time.

The Marques del Valle Hotel is right next to the cathedral. I'm familiar with Mexican churches and their interiors; I have always enjoyed the art in their stained-glass windows, their sculptures, bas-reliefs, murals made of diminutive ceramic tiles, and temple paintings. Sometimes the framed oil paintings speak of purity, too. Mexican religious art is soft and always has a touch of innocence that makes it much more interesting to me than the morbid darkness, the tortuous, contriving, asphyxiating feeling I associate with Spanish religious art.

This evening my attention goes first to the hundreds of candles inside. I'm not looking at the lighted ones, but the ones which refused to burn in church. Don Constantino told us that they are great allies to get rid of an enemy living adjacent to your land. You simply take those candles and light them on the boundary that separates the two properties. I find myself wondering how difficult is it to steal those candles in the sight of everyone since the church is always busy.

They are having the Mass in one of the wings of the building. It is there they have an image of Jesus Christ with an embroidered title that says: "Our Lord of the Thunderbolt." At the foot of the image there is a prayer to this lord. It is a marriage of pagan worship with Christian images. The Mixtecs are really worshipping their old god of thunderbolt who brings rain and abundance. I do not know if the Vatican would approve of what the priests and people of Oaxaca are doing, but I'm certain they would approve of the profound piety and deep faith of these people, the sincere warmth of their worship, and the pure place from where their prayers originate.

The priest is an old man who really feels what he is doing. The eyes of the people tell you everything about them. Tomorrow they might be sinners again, but today they are completely overtaken by the ceremony. They are pouring all that they are in the calling of the Lord.

Moved by the energy of the group I think about communion. I learned at a very early age that the worst sin is to partake of communion without confession. You are supposed to have a private time with the priest and tell him all the bad things you have done since the last time you took communion. Then he gives you a penance, usually a few prayers to clear you of sin, before eating the body of the Lord at the time of communion.

I look deep within myself to find out the sins I have committed since last time I took the host (ten years ago, forced by social pressure at the time of my religious wedding). Honestly, I could not find any. There is no shade of guilt or shame in my past. Am I that pure? A good Christian would say pride is my sin; I might be so blinded by my Luciferian arrogance that I don't recognize the rottenness of my human nature.

The fact is that I do recognize the baseness of my human nature, but after years of struggling with it, I learned to accept it, to live with it, to express it without harm to others, and even to enjoy it. That's why I never feel guilty about my past. Guilt might creep in sometimes when I feel I should be more of what I am now; but, this is a different kind of guilt, an internalized pressure to meet standards always remote and superhuman, but not of a moral nature.

So, if I feel happy with my little demons inside me, why should I be interested in taking communion? It is because I want to experience as close as possible a reconciliation with God from the Christian perspective.

After a long inner examination I conclude that I'm free of the sin of Satanic pride; then I decide to go for it, to partake of communion tonight. Besides, who is this poor old third-world fanatic dressed in religious robes in front of me to tell such a bright and learned man of the civilized world how to purify his crimes in the eyes of God. . . provided I had any?

I risked my soul's salvation by taking the host without previous confession. To tell you the truth, I felt Christ in my heart that evening. Not only that, I also saw the Holy Mother of God as expressed through the benevolent souls of those women Francisco Zuñiga immortalized in his sculptures all over the world. These women, fifty-to sixty-years old, with their hair in braids and their heads covered by shawls, with their oval bodies and their deep, melancholic eyes submerged in prayer at church or in the pure whiteness of their own minds when they perform the automatic activities that constitute their daily lives. . . they are Oaxaca's symbolic examples of the great universal mother. She lives in them and through them. The Mother of God breathes through these women all over the land of the Mixtecs.

That night I wash and cut in very tiny pieces the mushrooms bought in San José del Pacífico. I place them in a plastic bag.

The next morning my friends take me to the ruins of Monte Albán, the White Mountain, called Dani Baan or the Sacred Mountain, by the Zapotecs who built the temples there around 1000 B.C. I am going to eat the magic mushrooms there. The idea is risky because the whole operation is illegal. If I get crazy in a public place I might end up in jail. And boy! Monte Albán is a public place that day. There is no place to hide on such a fine Sunday morning.

Monte Albán is much older than Teotihuacán or any of the Mayan ruins. The Zapotecs had a hieroglyphic language and a numerical system 1500 years before the Mayans; they were the first ones to use the 260-day calendar Jose Arguelles attributes to the Mayans.

Monte Albán was a ceremonial center. They had no wars, and their blessed land—that still keeps a yearly temperature range of 90-50°F—provided them with all that they needed for a peaceful life. The Zapotecs were devoted to agriculture and the worship of their supreme invisible god, Pitao, and the minor deities of rain, thunder, corn, fertility, and so forth. The Zapotecs prospered for eighteen centuries, and then they disappeared as mysteriously as the later Toltecs and Mayans.

Some of the human figures in the bas-reliefs of Monte Albán resemble people suffering or with deformities. In the early years of the discovery of Monte Albán those figures were considered dancers, but the pain reflected in their facial expressions and their ungraceful, contorted bodies make contemporary archaeologists believe they represent sick people. Most likely the Sacred Mountain was not only a religious center, but it was also a healing place.

There is a spiritual warmth in the whole ancient city of the Zapotecs, and in some spots on the high pyramids I can feel impressive amounts of energy coming from the earth. I choose the top of one of the pyramids, the highest in the flat area, the one that looks down to the valley and the mountains from where the Mixtecs came once the Zapotecs had vanished. When I was walking up the stairs I had the fleeting image of a middle-aged priest twice human size at the top of the pyramid offering me a potion to drink in an earthenware cup.

Once my guides and I get to the top I check that no guards are in sight and take my own potion from my pocket. Then I wait for thirty minutes. The top of the pyramid is crowded with people, tourists, and locals that come and go. At first I fear that I might get out of balance because of them, but as time goes by I feel I can encompass all change within my being.

I then have insights on how the spiritual path has been understood in terms of progress, just as everything else in our civilization. Helped by the magic of the mushrooms and the ancient energy of the place, a whole new conception of growth, both spiritual and material, unfolds in my mind:

Our civilization is future-oriented; there is an inner rush to overlap present circumstances with higher achievements. The individual is understood and judged according to his/her power to be ahead of the race, always conquering, always expanding.

There is another way to be, much older, where what is important is the stability and peace naturally resulting from the awareness of the unity of all life. From this perception, going forward is a symptom of lack of connection with the source. The real achievement is to stay where you are and look deeply into the essence of your daily life. There you will find the magic of every moment, the oneness, the wholeness. You will be able to read the universal hologram in each one of its reflections in time and space.

I see how my next step on the path of enlightenment is to stop and forget about the path as a way to get from here to there. The radiation of eternal stability by means of beingness is what I should look for. . . by not looking for it.

I open my eyes after this short meditation and I see three women, each with a baby, in a triangle around me. The woman in front of me opens her blouse and without a trace of shame starts feeding the baby in her arms. This action is not as infrequent as it would be in a civilized country; Mexican Indians do this at times in public places. The real strangeness of the situation is that they are there, at the top of the pyramid. There is absolutely no reason for them to carry their babies on a dangerous and extenuating climb to stand up there only for a few moments. The sight of the woman and the baby in front of me brings to my memory the dream I had the night before my first experience with cosmic consciousness, eleven years ago...

I was twenty-five years old when I dreamed I was walking under a very dark night sky in a desolate flat landscape. I saw a shack that glowed with an amber light of its own, as if the substance it was made from owned this exquisite luminescence. I entered the small dwelling and a beautiful Mexican Indian woman with serene eyes was standing in the center of the room looking at me. I went toward her and knelt. She uncovered one of her breasts and pressed on it, bursting the whole Milky Way into my mouth. I entered an ecstatic trance that didn't go away after its power had awakened me. The next day I had a most profound cosmic experience during a ceremony held in a little valley in the mountains between the cities of Tijuana and Ensenada.

But now, at the top of the pyramid on the sacred mountain, I become aware I am standing in the center of a triangle of force built by the women. Were they conscious of what they were doing? Maybe they are not human entities, I thought; maybe they are the allies Carlos Castaneda writes about in some of his books. Maybe they are only a hallucination caused by the mushrooms. One of them says to the others, "The sun is coming. Let's go down." As the three of them begin their descent, I go to my guides to find out if the women were real. I notice I'm able to interact perfectly with everybody around me.

"Did you see those women?" I asked.

"Yes," my friends answer. "Did you notice that the three babies looked exactly alike? We were wondering if they were triplets and the other women were helping the mother that stood in front of you."

I knew then all that I needed to know. Real or not, the women were there synchronously to let me know about the omnipresence of the Great Mother whom I had recognized in my state of mystical exaltation in the church the night before.

I went back to my meditation. The vibration I was feeling went deeper. First, I thought I would connect with the archetype of the King, but I went beyond it to an area of consciousness where there is no sense of separation from others. Everything blends in a center of peace.

From this state I went out to speculate about life in Zapotec times. I could feel how the Zapotecs had a very different view of life; in the many centuries of peace their theocratic government provided them with whatever they needed because their needs were few and simple.

I felt the spirits of the high priests and priestesses of Monte Albán as immortal and enlightened, concentrating from higher dimensions into those narrow coordinates of time and space as bees in a hive with the purpose of shaping the raw consciousness of that emerging civilization. Perhaps these spirits wanted to help young souls grow into an awareness of their own immortality.

I felt the cosmic teachers knowing when the cycle was over, taking the graduated disciples with them, and leaving future generations under a government of hollow shells of priests, shallow personalities with a taste for power and ceremony. I felt the gradual disintegration of the remnants of the Zapotec civilization in a process that took centuries. And then I perceived how the Mixtecs came over the land, not as conquerors, but as another group-mind looking for its place in life, looking for the manifestation and the blossoming of those qualities the spirit had bestowed upon its unified consciousness in the abstract regions of timelessness.

We stay in Monte Albán for two hours and the magic potion does not interfere with my physical activities. We walk through the ruins and I can feel some of the layers of memories the ancient stones of that place have preserved to the present.

My psychic stability makes me think that the effect of the potion is not as strong as it should be. Maybe the dosage was not right, I think. A little discouraged by the lack of drama, and feeling embarrassed to keep my friends in the direct sunlight without anything to do, I tell them that the journey is over and now we can go anywhere they want. They decide to take me to a popular restaurant outside the city.

The restaurant is so crowded we can hardly walk in. After eating one piece of fish the effect of the mushrooms becomes stronger and I excuse myself to walk alone in the flat land that surrounds the restaurant.

There I hear the little voices in choral harmony again: "See? We told you! We are with you now. Now we can talk. We would like you to write a book about life, about how to experience life, how to live to the fullest expression of what a human can be. It should be a book on how to deal with mystery, how to realize the vulnerability of the human condition, and then step into the mouth of the universal snake, risking life in the process of living. A book to let others know how to open themselves to joys and tribulations, to teach others how to accept pleasure and pain in the unavoidable process of unfoldment. A book on awakening. A book on having courage in an ocean of fear. A book on stepping into a typhoon to find the center of peace. A book on how to walk in the labyrinth of life which is the universal serpent's body, and how to get to its heart, which is always warm."

I feel exhilarated; bliss pours from the center of my brain. My friends have finished dinner and are calling me now.

Feeling in perfect control of myself, I ask my friends to take me to the hotel. I had read that the effect of *Psilocybin* mushrooms lasts about six hours. It's been five hours since I took them and it shouldn't be long before I feel perfectly clear. . . or so I think. . .

On returning to the hotel waves of bliss run through my body. I go to my room, lie on the bed, and then the real journey begins! My body moves like a serpent in the bed. It is a very pleasurable sensation, as if the body is discharging years of control from the rational mind. Icons of diverse animals run through my mind's screen in ochers and sepias, reminding me of prehistoric cave paintings. I feel diverse animal impulses rushing through my body. I realize that the drives of animal and human species can be perceived as non-local currents of energy with lives of their own, abstract forces that exist in the transpersonal levels of consciousness and come into manifestation to and through physical beings by means of feeling, finding expression in the actions and reactions of the species of the planet.

The little choral voices appear to tell me that all those currents of life should be allowed to come through. They respond to higher cyclical laws and are closer to the source. They are as sacred as anything else; these pre-human psychic dynamisms were created by the same one God. The voices of the mushrooms tell me it is good to think of God as a playful, happy child; this allows expression to those currents without hindrance from the mental structures created by social programming.

The voices now ask me to eat the dried mushrooms that I have gotten from Don Constantino. I do it. Then I have a sudden panic attack. What if this is too much? What if I do a crazy thing such as going out naked in the streets or yelling like a maniac in my room until they break the door and take me to a mental institution? What if I can't control myself and they take me to jail?

(I have heard terrible stories about Mexican jails. Everybody says they are worse than hell.) I see my fears as red devils, with tridents and all, coming to my room from everywhere, like violent scavengers in the sight of food.

"We fooled you! We fooled you!" said the little voices. "We needed to do it. It's for your own good. We waited until you believed in us and now that you are alone we are going to release our full effect. Now we are going to heal you."

My right hand moves with a will of its own. It is massaging a very precise spot on my left wrist. During the last few days I have been feeling a dull pain in my wrist which I have associated since nine years ago with changes in barometric pressure and weather. I always thought the pain was coming from a small bump that appeared after I almost dislocated my hand in a basketball mishap. Now my right hand is rubbing with force and determination the real source of the pain, a very small area about one inch away from the bump.

The little voices change into one deep feminine voice with the melody and power of a waterfall. The voice tells me that she is going to release stagnant energy associated with repression of my instinctive nature. As my right hand rubs on, the fear takes form, and then I see images of my childhood—my father in one of his frequent anger explosions. I notice how my apprehension those days set into activity a program for early maturation that too soon overrode the happy playful nature of a child's mind. The seriousness of my behavior was reinforced by praise, and soon I became the little genius, the little educated puppet who learned to play the game of society for the reward of admiration.

The fear is experienced almost as intensely as when I was a child, but the voice is comforting me at the same time. It sounds like an expert doctor who is telling me about how the blocked energy has surfaced in the physical world as the accident in my wrist, and how some of the channels of energy in the body have a lot to release. It keeps massaging my wrist until it uncovers

My life was going well at that time. I was practicing yoga and Egyptian ceremonial magic. I had a girlfriend and was earning enough money to survive. My only aim in life was to attain cosmic consciousness. I was absolutely committed to doing whatever was necessary to get there. I found after the meeting that from all the members of the group, only Ramón and I were willing to put Carlos's teachings into practice.

Carlos invited us to meet again with some of the witches of his party. He took us to a park and later to a Japanese restaurant. Three women came along with him. I felt a strong connection with one of them, an anthropologist who recently had been released from being kidnapped by a shaman in the Peruvian jungle. She had lots of energy; courage radiated from her eyes. She was introduced to me as Gina. She seemed to be curious about me. Soon after that I did a ceremony in my temple and felt her attached to my neck, watching me. I could even talk to her and hear her answers. I liked her energy and was curious about this phenomenon, but didn't like her ability to intrude telepathically into my energy field. I decided to have a friendly challenge to find out if I could clear her out of my mind. I did my magical banishings, but they were ineffective. The next morning the feeling of her presence was gone. Later, without any comment on my part, Carlos told me the witches had been checking me in their sorcery dreaming and they liked me.

Around that time during one of my magical ceremonies held in my basement temple, I felt Don Juan coming into my telepathic awareness. I tried to dismiss the intrusive voice in my head, but he didn't go. He offered to give me proof of his presence by teaching me a magical technique to materialize something in my life. This technique involved the use of flour and water in the creation of a magical necklace.

Still feeling this mental contact might have been a trick of my own mind, I asked in a partly challenging, partly joking way, "What can I do with this procedure to prove you are a real contact tonight?"

3

CARLOS CASTANEDA AND THE WARRIOR'S EAGLE

At the end of 1981, Ramón, a friend of mine living in Los Angeles, told me about one of his friends who was meeting with Carlos Castaneda in a vegetarian restaurant owned by a yoga association. Castaneda gave him his P.O. box number, and now Ramón was passing it on to me. I wrote to Carlos asking him for an interview; a few days later Ramón told me that Carlos was coming to talk to a small group of people and I was invited. This happened before my letter arrived.

At the time of the meeting Carlos talked about the need to erase the personal history and banish routines and ties that prevented full expression of freedom. He also taught us an exercise. It was about being absolutely conscious of every act, no matter how ordinary, as an expression of personal will.

masters sitting on those benches, dressed like everyone else. Perhaps something happened there and I missed it. Looking at those benches I feel intrigued...distressed. A week later I would be walking in Montreal. A friend of mine would take me to a bookstore where I would buy the only book of Carlos Castaneda I hadn't read. My heart would beat in surprise and anxiety when I learn from that book that in that same plaza the great Mexican *nagual* Don Juan gave Carlos the last lessons in the way to total freedom, specifically those of teletransportation, a phenomena that came to my mind as an obsession all the time I spent in Oaxaca.

This discovery triggered in full force the memories of my meetings and conversations with Carlos Castaneda in California eleven years ago and its resulting influence on my life.

something like an insect stuck to the inside of my wrist. It looks to my psychic sight like a black ant the size of a big cockroach, but its function is more like a tick. It is holding onto an energy channel running through my wrist.

I realize this parasite is the representation of the negative blockage and decide to play psychic surgeon: I project a laser beam of psychic energy with my right hand toward the psychic tick, but I can't create any change. It is as if the energy I send belongs to a dimension different from that of the insect. The voice tells me to use the tweezers in my toiletry bag. This is a big surprise for me since I never carry tweezers on my trips. But then the shadow of a memory crosses my mind and I decide to give it a try. Yes! the hair removers are in my toiletry bag. Most probably I placed them there unconsciously, or maybe the voice of wisdom, knowing what was ahead, whispered in my ear the subliminal command. Or maybe the tweezers were teletransported the moment I looked for them. Who knows? With the tweezers I pluck the intruder with the same discomfort and ease of that of a real tick. Now the voice recommends that I wear a copper bracelet over that area.

The fear subsides, but it is not gone yet. I hear the voice informing me that the fear is also stored in my spine. I see then six Indian healer women chanting to me: "The little boy is scared. He was born scared. We are going to heal him. Peace, Peace." The melody is like a nursery rhyme. They are offering comfort to the inner child.

During the whole session in the hotel there are two things that keep coming to my mind. All the time I open my eyes I see the forged iron ornament that holds the naked lightbulb over my head. I see there the exquisite body of a black goddess with serpents around her and an open flower bursting from her heart. It has a seductive power that is inviting me to life. . .to life.

I keep looking through the window to the plaza. I have the feeling that it is a magical place. Perhaps there are mysterious

"Use it to make money," the voice of Don Juan answered. "If you don't get from your next client three times what you are used to, I am a worthless ghost."

"If it works and I want to contact you again, how should I proceed?" I asked. "We only come when we want to; we are not like your Egyptian gods. We cannot be summoned. I came this time only to give you proof of our existence."

Shortly after I followed the procedures to create the magical necklace, I received a call from a new customer. It goes without saying that Don Juan was correct.

During the physical meetings with Carlos I made it very clear to him that I had decided to cut with everything and go in search of total freedom. In the next weeks Carlos called me on the phone several times, telling me things such as: "You are the best of the group... The witches and I like you a lot... You are ready." When I inquired about the other members of the group who met with him, he answered that they were not ready, not even Ramón. (Later I found out he was playing the same trick on Ramón, telling him that he was the only one worthy of his attention, that I was too stuck to my Egyptian practices, and losing energy because of the relationship with my girlfriend.)

In our last meeting he gave me personal advice in the form of general information. However, I couldn't understand at the time its personal meaning. He told me that Don Juan explained to him that people who are the "last-borns" of a family do not have enough "glands" to be independent, and always attach to others to drain their energy. He told me that Don Juan asked him to cross to the other side of the street whenever he would see a "glandless" one coming his way. He was right about my girlfriend!

Over the phone he invited me to come on one of his trips, or so I thought. I was so excited! I told my family and my girlfriend that I was leaving without knowing when I would return. I prepared myself and bought my Greyhound ticket to meet him at the appointed time in Los Angeles. Then he called me on the eve of our departure. First, he asked if I were ready. I told him I was. Then he told me he had to go to New York to defend himself against a panel of anthropologists who were writing a book against him, and that as soon as he returned from his trip he would call me to continue with our plans.

I spent months waiting for him. The anxiety of everyday changed into the feeling that somehow I had been disqualified, that perhaps some stupid thing I had said over the phone was the reason for that. I felt worthless, wasted. It was my only aspiration in life, now shattered, and it was my fault. Never in my life had I felt that I could not meet the given standards, no matter how difficult. I felt devastated.

But something else was happening in my dreams. I was dreaming with him almost every night! Somewhere along the line I started to understand the pattern. In his last call he told me something that did not make sense to me until much later: "Luisito, you and I are like two pirates. When pirates cross in the ocean they just say 'bye' to each other." Somehow he was giving me credit for something, as if he were telling me I could be independent and still make it. It was clear from these sentences that he was not considering a permanent contact between us as was my hope those days. So, to heal the pain of rejection and to make sense of his disappearance in my life, I interpreted his words on the pirate world to mean that I belonged to another school of development on the inner planes, and he had only given me a push along the way.

A push? He had propelled me with such force that I could hardly stay on my feet...or should I say in my right mind? I thought I was going crazy. Something terrible happened to me as the power of his magical gift unfolded in my world.

At the time of our last meeting in Los Angeles he gave me a copy of his recently released hardbound edition of *The Eagle's Gift*. I remember him holding the book close to his heart for a second or two before he gave it to me. Later, he went on talking with someone else in my presence about how Don Juan had taught him to sleep with the books he had to study as a way to absorb their essence more than read them in a linear way. Of course, I slept with the book beneath my pillow every night until its power was released and I could not keep it in my sight anymore.

Another apparently irrelevant act by Carlos should have warned me that the book was a powerful magical gift. I was about to write down the address of someone I had met in the same group on the inside cover of his book when he took it from my hands and hurriedly looked for a piece of paper inside his pockets. He gave me the piece of paper, asking me not to write on the book. I could not make sense of this. I even thought it might have involved just some kind of personal pride to keep his book looking neat. I was so dumb!

Those days I was about to open a school of applied metaphysics in Tijuana, México. I painted a beautiful Egyptian mural, bought all the necessary furniture, and made myself ready to become the teacher. I had enough experience as an instructor of yoga, astrology, and Tarot symbolism to impress anybody interested. I had a very high concept of myself in those days...but something inside was making me feel miserable, and I could not find out what it was.

The day I finished decorating my classroom I checked the Tarot for the potential success of my undertaking. Terrible cards appeared so I performed a ritual to change the room's vibrations. The cards came out all good this time and I felt secure; but, in the afternoon, upon entering the classroom again, I recognized a foul psychic atmosphere.

I knew then that something was wrong. How could I know what it was? Since I felt a desperate need to confront the obstacle, I performed an intense ceremony that night. It consisted of cutting the skin in the middle of my chest to obtain a drop of blood then offered to Horus, the Egyptian god of war and vengeance, to once and forever clean away all the darkness inside oneself. During the ceremony I focused my will on the unbending intent of seeing God face to face, even if I died.

Horus is represented in Egyptian mythology as a hawk. No hawk came to my call, but the most-fearsome universal presence of an eagle seemed to pervade everywhere I focused my mind. It was the shamanic eagle of all traditions, the imperial eagle of many past and present warrior civilizations. Because there was a Nazi overtone to the energy, I felt very strongly that rituals of this kind had been done by the high officers of the SS during World War II.

It was more than anything else the eagle of the sorcerers in Don Juan's world, in total dominion, with unlimited power over all living beings. There was no escape because the eagle was everywhere. It extended to infinity behind every crack in the barriers that the rational individual mind erects and reinforces every day to sustain individualized consciousness. I felt it would swallow the universe in the end. I felt the only escape against the eagle was to be dead already. The pain of knowing that destruction is at hand, no matter when, I experienced as unbearable.

I could only see separation, destruction, isolation in this vision. I instinctively knew that to go through this vision I needed to reconcile the nightmare I was in with other aspects of my life, but it was impossible to do so at this time. The eagle's vision eclipsed any other perceptions of existence; my mind was shattered. The eagle's gift was the gift of loneliness, of cold detachment from any emotional drive. . .the life of the living dead.

It was a rite of passage into manhood, a military initiation into the crudeness of life. Life with no glamor, no illusions, no hopes, no expectations. The warrior's archetype to its extreme maleness, bordering on cruelty. No trace of love could be found in the universe I was ensnared in, and I could never return to the comfortable safety of ignorance. I was cursed by this knowledge for the rest of my life.

At the same time the eagle was eating me as its prey, I was trapped in its claws. It ate me slowly, with indifference, and at the same time it was showing me all my neurotic traits: how I had lived out all my life inside an artificial bubble created by my rigid and shallow perception. I had built a cocoon for protection, the cocoon of petty thoughts wrapped about a self-centered life. Now it was crushed.

Since the eagle had eaten me I was nothing more than a mere shadow in the world of sleeping ones. They can dream their illusions, have their hopes and fears, but I had no right to do so. The curse of the eagle would make me fly alone from peak to peak. If I stayed in a single place too long, everything would be shattered by the eagle's claws. People would come and go out of my life; feelings would not hold. My inner fire would consume every nest I built.

The eagle told me: "Do not build anything. If you bury yourself in the petty illusions of a regular life, I will come in seven years and destroy all your life. Do not hold to any aim, even an interest in achieving spiritual liberation should be destroyed because every desire is an impurity at this stage in your development. Only when you don't care about the crossing of the Veil of Manifestation anymore will you have crossed it."

All the time I was having these visions I felt as if I were a neurotic worm in the face of infinity. All my delusions about my heroic quest to conquer spiritual reality and help the world were shattered. I learned that my personality was but an aberrant particle of consciousness that was deluding itself into believing it was the center of the universe. There was a bitterness in the realization that my juvenile dreams, my candid intentions, were to no avail anymore in this ruthless world I had entered.

I felt as if the eagle were pulling me by the hair and showing me without mercy scenes of unbearable crudeness and desolation.

In real life only results count; I didn't have any. I felt guilty that in my twenty-five years I had been missing the train of reality dreaming neurotic fantasies that I would not reach at all. I felt ashamed that all the efforts in my past to find transcendence were just wasted time.

I was seeing fields of horrendous destruction, afterwards landscapes of pain and ruin. At the same time I felt I was learning a lesson in reality: the world as it really is when one's perception is not clouded by emotional sentimentalism. The Nietzschean philosophy was absolute truth from this level. The Nazi phenomenon was a manifestation of the power of the eagle, lurking eternally behind every crack in the shelters of humanity's infantile understanding of existence.

I saw generations of human beings digging their fragile trenches against the implacable advance of the eagle's claws; human affection, plans for the future, recreation of every kind were only shields to avoid seeing the horror of life. Destruction was the only certainty. Death always the end.

Yes, there was the possibility of transcending this law, but to focus on the ideal of the magus beyond life and death was at this stage only another brittle mental construction to entertain the mind and distract it from reality. I had better open my eyes and confront fully and honestly the visions the eagle was rubbing in my face. The visions were so sharp they were piercing, as blades slicing into my soul.

Many times I thought of breaking the ceremony's momentum by running up to the house where the distractions of the human world and my parents' help would soothe the shock of the visions. But I decided to resist and grow, although the direction of my growth was uncertain to me. This ceremony of initiation into manhood was indeed long overdue; I was not being circumcised or tortured by the adults in my tribe as usually happens, but the pain in my mind was as much as I was able to endure without breaking into chaos.

Most of religion is emotional sentimentalism. Gnosis eliminates this.

THE HEART OF THE SERPENT

I stayed in my temple all night. Before falling asleep I had a vision that my brain had been removed and a large iridescent crystal sphere had been installed inside my skull.

The next morning I had an impressive energy—raw, dark, and very intense. The lovebirds that my mother kept were terrified at my sight. Even when I was three yards from their cage they threw themselves in panic against the bars as I looked at them. I was acting like a robot—aloof, detached, but in complete control of my actions. I felt great! But there was an underlying feeling that something big, and not too pleasant, was about to happen.

Four days later, I was writing in my magic diary about the whole eagle experience, when I saw a white dot of very brilliant light floating in the air, coming into the center of my vision. I had seen that brilliant spark many times before, but always from out of the corner of my eyes. This was the first time this light being wanted to convey a message. I focused on it and the overwhelming sensation that a happening of great magnitude was about to occur came over me.

I finished the record of my ceremony and then reaffirmed the magical oath that is part of the Horus invocation I used at that time. The oath was about giving the God of Light all your blood—to the last drop. It is believed that once you gave your life to the sun when it is reborn at dawn, you would become part of him, and operate as a warrior of light, detached from the human traits that hinder the success of your endeavors.

Upon signing the magical oath I felt a sudden rush of anxiety take over my body. It was as if the god, a sudden reality now, was hungry for my blood. It was all right, I thought, to go ahead and keep my promise. I knew the magical oath was a symbol of one's resolution in the process of enlightenment. The scary part was that the god now appeared in his most-primitive form: the ultimate tyrant in the universe, sucking life from his servants, living from century to century on his victims' feelings of terror, abasement, and defeat.

This I knew I had to fight with body, mind, and soul. I should not become a slave. But the dynamic energy of this malignant set of stresses on the transpersonal level of consciousness was jolting my nervous system like a puppet. It was a powerful thoughtform built by the war rites of all cultures. It was thirsty for blood and submission. I had opened the door and now was unable to send it back to the abyss from which it came.

The anxiety attacks continued; I was obsessed with paranoid feelings about this cosmic oppressor. If I had allowed myself to express fear, I would have cried like a rat. My body was sweating profusely. My first idea was to discharge the excess of energy in my system by means of physical exertion.

I ran around the block several times, wishing to find a reason to engage in a fight and distract my troubled mind in the heat of physical challenge. I jumped rope and practiced karate kicks and blows until exhausted. But the psychic pressure did not dissipate.

At night I called A——, my teacher in matters of magic. He explained to me that this contact with the dweller on the threshold would probably manifest first on the mental level, but later it would work its way into my emotional nature, and finally be grounded in physical events. He recommended that I take extra showers to change the electrical charge in my brain and a couple of medicinal herbal teas to keep my nervous system as stable as possible given the circumstances.

The days that followed were a constant battle to keep my sanity. I had sudden attacks of anxiety, and thoughts of supreme arrogance, isolation, violence, and ruthless destruction, as well as the tendency to avoid the pain and tension of the fight by selling my soul once and forever to become the slave of that eagle demon.

I knew I was facing the dark side of the god of light, but all my knowledge of analytical psychology and of magic was inadequate to deal with the powerful unconscious death currents I had unchained from hell. The worst part of this nightmare was that I did not know whether this psychic contact was positive; maybe my negative revulsion toward it was based on the fear of giving up my old views of life and truly transforming my personality in the crucible of spiritual fire. Maybe I was perceiving a spiritual being through the distorted views of a neurotic mind. Maybe it was all my fault.

I lost all emotional drive. I could see no transcendence in human existence; life was devoid of meaning and I was unable to find any. There was no place to go, no aim to work toward, no pleasure to look for. My heart was paralyzed. I did not want to kill myself simply because I felt that hopelessness would be even more intense on the other side.

Whenever I tried to see inside, to find the nucleus that had defined my sense of self all my life, I found only emptiness. The most-central part of me had gone. I envisioned this part of my soul as a cowardly hermit crab flying in panic at the sight of the eagle, leaving only the shell, the carcass of my automatic reflexes, to deal with the event. I could have no concept of myself. I honestly did not know who I was anymore.

Even during the worst days I always seemed perfectly normal to others. The only thing that demonstrated my nightmare was the sudden appearance of sweat on my hands whenever I had the vision of the cosmic abyss open in front of me, sucking me into nothingness. I never looked for professional help. I knew no Mexican psychologist would understand what was going on. My confidants where my mother and my girlfriend. I might have talked to other friends if I had any, but I lost them because of a strange incident that made me a fearful presence among them.

This happened two days after the vision of the eagle, two days before I realized the danger I was in. Ramón invited me to Tecate, a small city two hours from Tijuana. As we discussed our experiences with the Castaneda philosophy along the way, we both saw a big cloud the size of the horizon first becoming the head of the hawk god of the Egyptians, and then the head of a raven. On our way back we drove to the skirts of Colorado Mountain, east of Tijuana. Ramón took out of his car a cannabis cigarette. He smoked three joints. He was trying to access higher states of awareness using whatever means he had available those days.

I had experimented with cannabis in the past, always in my temple, and never for recreation. I could not find anything transcendental from its use, and rejected it as a vehicle to the higher worlds. For me it only exacerbated the inner dialogue that keeps our world together. Perhaps it could give new angles of vision, but never go beyond the boundaries of the mind. Besides, I hated to feel stupid and ordinary when the effects were wearing off. I refused to smoke, as I always did those days.

I offered to give Ramón a push with my etheric force to help him step out of his body and reach higher worlds. I recommended that he squat for a minute, then stand up with the firm resolution of flying above his body, while at the same time keeping his physical balance. The sky was clouded above us.

When Ramón jumped up to a standing position I used my will to project his consciousness as high as I could imagine. A tremendous force emanated from me as I went into a brief altered state of consciousness. When I opened my eyes, I saw a hole in the clouds just above us, and Ramón unconscious on the ground. A second later he rose with the ability of a dancer. He brushed off his jeans with the palms of his hands and asked me:

"What happened?"

"Just what I said. I pushed you out. What did you feel?"

"I don't know. What do you think about all this?"

"I didn't like the fact that you fell on the ground. I know that when you are stoned you get dizzy when you stand up suddenly, but I have always managed to keep my balance when I practiced this technique in the past."

"I don't know. What do you think about all this?"

"I think we did something. Look at the hole in the clouds. Maybe you went through there."

"I don't know. What do you think about all this?"

"I don't know. I wonder if you can remember what happened in the middle of your blackout."

"I don't know. What do you think about all this?"

"Can you tell me something about your experience?"

"I don't know. What do you think about all this?"

At this point I knew something was wrong with Ramón. He kept repeating this loop of words for the rest of the day. I offered to drive his car back home, but he refused. The descent was dangerous and he even pretended he had lost control of the car's brakes just to scare me. These were the only times when he broke his cyclic sentence. He repeated, "I don't know. What do you think about all this?" at least a hundred times before we reached my house. I offered to come out with something for him to eat to help ground him. When I returned he had gone.

Several days later I got the rest of the story from our friends at the Supreme Order of Aquarius, an association of vegetarians with interest in yoga, astrology, and a mixture of New Age grandeur, theosophical philosophy, and an evangelical tendency for service.

I had been the director of one of their esoteric schools. After resigning my position, all my circle of esoteric friends were still there. When Ramón arrived at the headquarters they were having a lecture. He exhibited there another strange cyclic pattern that caught the attention of our friends. Ramón looked so disoriented that they thought he was under the influence of LSD. Our compassionate friends decided to save his reputation by taking him to a hotel. Before they left him there they found out he had been with me. The next day one of them called to find out what happened. He sounded polite, but there was a note of indignation in his voice; they believed I had given Ramón a strong hallucinogenic.

They accepted my explanation about the energy push, yet I knew I was responsible for all this to a good degree because I had not taken into account the increased power at my disposal after the eagle ceremony. I would not have been able to produce such an intense effect under normal circumstances.

Days later some of them came to my house to find out more about what I had done to Ramón, so I read to them my record of the eagle experience. Now they had double reason to be horrified: Ramón was living proof of my evil arts. He had no recollection of the whole trip to Tecate, up to the afternoon of the next day when he awakened in the hotel room where he had been placed. My morbid record of the magical ceremony was sufficient evidence to them of the dangers of my unconscious levels. I had been their leader in the past; but now, outside the safety of the Supreme Order of Aquarius, I was not a reliable guide, not even a friend anymore.

For months before the eagle experience, I had dreams about forces of an abyss coming to attack the city I defended on the top of a mountain, or terrible conflagrations of fire destroying my natal city, or lightning bolts partially destroying our family's library room. After the eagle experience I sometimes dreamed that I was in trouble, but I was always helped by simple people from rural México. Often they were women.

Many of those dreams were conscious dreams with Carlos Castaneda or his teachers. In one of those conscious dreams I was being pulled from the area around my navel—a very physical, almost painful sensation—by something that looked like a cable. I knew that Don Juan was at the other end of the cable taking me to another dimension. I was being dragged into a universe of yellow light, things resembling gigantic machinery were all around. I woke up trying to endure the distressful sensation and reach the other side to see Don Juan's face.

In another of these dreams I was with a group of apprentices where Carlos taught us how to call the power of the wind by drawing a big "V" on the ground, the arrowhead shape following the direction of the wind. The converging lines in the ground would act as a condenser of the wind's power. It was just a matter of stepping into the point where the lines met to absorb and channel that power. In that dream I was acting like an infatuated magician's apprentice, showing off my ability to call this power to levitate and move like a clown only a few inches above the ground. Carlos pretended to be amused, but I saw in his face his impatience with my childish display.

In the days that followed the eagle's encounter, my dreams with Carlos were very healing. He was teaching me the art of stalking as a way to keep grounded in the middle of my psychic turbulence. In one of those dreams he was taking me to visit somebody; he was at the wheel of an old pickup truck and asked me to get in. On entering the vehicle I got a stain of ink on my shirt. Looking at its origin I discovered the dripping ink was some kind of fool's trap Carlos had arranged to teach me how important it was to be fully aware and focused in the present.

Then we drove to an uninviting gray house. Carlos violently called the attention of the people inside, then hid himself to let me suddenly deal with the inquiring look of the man who came out of the house with an uninviting, almost bitter expression on his face. I was left there with no time to formulate an excuse for the noise caused by Carlos. Certainly this was another lesson to force me to put my full attention on the matter at hand.

At other times these conscious dreams were an almost hilarious proof of the certainty of my astral state. Several times, upon discovering I was in a dream, I rushed to Carlos to let him know I knew I was no good at keeping myself in this precarious state of awareness, begging him to instruct me as soon as possible because I was afraid I would wake up at any moment.

In my last conscious dream with Carlos during that period, he came to me with his face painted half-black and half-white. He told me that this was the last dream in which we would meet, that I was too old to continue with his teachings. I was twenty-six years old at the time. I woke up crying, as if I had lost my best friend.

Before meeting with Carlos I had hundreds of dreams where I threw myself off a cliff to fly, or tried to dissolve myself into an exquisite golden glow as prelude to awakening. I leapt from the cliff in regular dreams as well as in conscious dreams to the point where I always consciously looked for the cliff upon discovering my awareness in the dream state. The jump from the cliff became a regular feature of most of my conscious dreams for several years. After meeting with Carlos and the eagle's experience this dream stopped.

My last physical communication with Carlos was a letter I sent to him. I thanked him for his magical gift. I said I had met the eagle and I knew I was not able to integrate its force yet. I humbly confessed I would need several years to integrate the whole experience. Although my letter sounded polite and organized, the truth was I was scared to death to meet with Carlos again. I needed all the safety of my family and my home as a barricade against the eagle's continuous attack. The next years of my life were a long and painful climb out of distress.

4
CLIMBING OUT OF THE ABYSS

@@@@@@@@@@@@@@@@@@@@

It took me about six months to get out of psychic danger, three years to learn to feel like a regular human being, and nine years to assimilate the whole experience with the eagle.

I had a few signposts that gave me hope along the way. One year before the eagle experience, A——, my teacher of magic, had done a psychic reading of my spiritual path, and had seen my path going into the Great Abyss where the light of the spiritual goal was not seen anymore. He heard the voice of Isis telling me that at that time my task would be to walk unremittingly, trusting that the commitment to harmony I had made in the past would act as a thread in the maze of darkness. The Goddess told my teacher that my destiny would not be as difficult after that ordeal, that I would receive a tree of gold and green as a symbol of growth and productivity.

I had a conscious dream in which Merlin was scrutinizing me very closely. Then he took me out into the stratosphere and pointed to a city three hours from Tijuana, telling me, "Wait until they call you to institute a palace of justice. When you work on political matters, your next stage will be fulfilled." Effectively, four years later I was called to teach metaphysics in that city. The last meeting I had with my students there was a time during elections. We performed a very successful magical ritual to change the political direction of the state. The next week the corrupted party that had kept power for the last sixty years, by trick and force, lost the elections for the first time.

Even during the darkest days of my recovery from the eagle's experience I still retained those memories of states of cosmic consciousness and fusion with infinity I had experienced in the past. My yogic experience helped keep me in balance. There was a small part of me who trusted that this psychological state was only one of the many angles of understanding revealed in the process of enlightenment.

My only resolution for the time being was to apply myself to doing whatever I found myself doing—to the best of my abilities. I put myself to doing grounding tasks, such as cleaning the house and gardening, as well as helping my father's employees in the manufacture of plexiglass and neon signs. To develop my concentration and my will I practiced archery every day.

I decided to get reeducated in human feelings and, I know one may laugh at this, but I took up the tedious task of watching three soap operas per day. It was a complete surprise to me to find out how much of my old rigid self I had lost. I always mocked those ridiculous dramas; now I was crying and laughing like an innocent soul.

My sleep brought peace; my days were full of tension, as if the inclement eye of Horus were watching me all the time, with military judgment, ready to punish me over the most insignificant mistake. I knew I was perceiving life from behind a screen of cruelty, part of my shadow. I recognized this pattern of cosmic paranoia and after a few days decided to play challenging games with the angry God. I would say, "Oh yeah! Let's see if you're so powerful you can torture me if I do this!" Then I would act in some funny way contrary to my ordinary behavior.

For years after the eagle experience I woke up with an aura of misery and discomfort that I set myself to purify every day. A——, my magical mentor, wrote an inspired document about my situation that gave me enough clues to work out a metaphysical conceptual understanding of my position on the path. He channeled the Avatar of Synthesis, who recommended I should unite the vision of the eagle with the vision of the lion. This recommendation was based on Hermetic philosophy as given in the esoteric teachings corresponding to the fourteenth Major Arcanum of the Tarot, where you see an angel blending fire and water. He is flanked by a lion and an eagle, representing complementary forces of nature that should become one to accomplish spiritual work. In my particular case the eagle represented the cold, detached nature of the mind; the lion became the symbol for the nobility and courage of the heart.

From this I devised mental exercises to blend the energies of the Third Eye and heart chakras: I imagined a universal lion climbing a mountain to an eagle's nest where he met and fought with the great bird until the two fused into a rainbow-colored griffin.

For the first year I was unable to meditate or to practice rituals. Every attempt to still my mind or to connect with the transcendental levels brought an unbearable inrush of energy. Whenever I meditated I developed anxiety. I was ungrounded and I knew it.

My emotions were playing tricks on me; I had painful waves of awareness of the negative side of my family's psychodynamics and how it affected me unconsciously. Some mornings I woke up with insights into how my father had always given me freedom of thought, but had been absent emotionally, almost cruelly by virtue of his detachment. How my mother had given me all her love, but also her fears and her overbearing, suffocating presence. How the high expectations imposed on me drove me to feel I was different from anyone else, and how I learned to meet those expectations by applying myself to mysticism and magic. How my mother's impatience and ignorance had pushed me into school too young to meet the physical challenges of the other boys, so that my first social experiences were tainted by feelings of inferiority and fear.

From these insights I developed a more mature vision of myself: I could understand my spiritual ambitions as the result of an imperfect psychological growth within an unbalanced family environment. I was not the spiritual hero I had fashioned myself to be. My ideas about myself changed and I became more sensible and realistic. This new way of perceiving life helped me to integrate human affections and feel more of my human nature.

I directed my efforts toward becoming an ordinary person. I never opened the applied metaphysics school; I was living proof metaphysics didn't work to create a better life. I could no longer teach something I was trying to avoid. I married an ordinary girl and she became my guide in matters of mediocrity. I did the best I could, and this was my mistake. While living with her I fooled myself into believing the whole eagle affair had been the turning point of my life, and now all that was left for me to do was to work, have children, grow old, and die. I simply shrugged my shoulders and accepted this fate. What I didn't know at the time was that the spiritual spark was still there—buried beneath the ashes of the great conflagration.

I devoted all my will to achieving harmony in my new home and things went well for two years. I sold most of my books on metaphysics. I became a teacher and then the director of the graphic-design department in a prestigious university. I was also working with private clients. Those were some of the most difficult times for the Mexican economy, but my added sense of realism helped me to earn a decent living.

Slowly, imperceptibly at first, my fiery nature was coming back to life. Little by little I devoted more and more time to spiritual disciplines and guiding meditation groups scattered throughout the city. My wife didn't like it. Her jealousy and my inner split clashed. We had quarrels that I always lost, promising again and again I would stop devoting time to occupations outside our common goals, only to find later that I couldn't keep myself from my fascination with the esoteric, the occult, the mystic, the transcendental. In my mind I was committed to our family life, but my spirit had other plans and I could not recognize them. I didn't want to. The truth is that I knew how all this would end, but I did not want to believe it.

Several years before, when we first talked about marriage she proposed to me. I answered: "I'm not sure. Let's ask the I Ching." [The Chinese book of divination.]

"Are you crazy?" she said.

"No, I don't feel clear. Saying no might mean I'm afraid of commitment; saying yes might mean I am yielding to your inner urge without hearing my own."

"I think you are a coward for not making a decision by yourself."

"But you also think I'm a coward if I say I don't want to marry, so from your viewpoint I have only one way to demonstrate my courage."

"You are confusing me. This is only wordplay. Don't you love me?"

"Yes, but marriage entails many other things."

"So you'd rather keep safe in your Mommy's house than assume your responsibilities in life?"

"See? That's psychological pressure. That's the kind of emotional blackmail I don't want to yield to."

"Okay, since you don't really care if you marry or not, why don't you just marry me?"

"Because I believe there is higher wisdom that I can't access now. That's why I want to consult the I Ching."

"Okay, I just hope you can keep to the I Ching 'decision' once it is given."

I got Hexagram 44, which represents a female line introducing itself into a solid block of five masculine lines. The literal Chinese translation in the book I consulted read: "The maiden comes to marry. She is powerful. One should not marry such a maiden."

It goes without saying that she hates the I Ching up to this day.

Months later, disregarding the wise advice of the marital oracle, I married out of a feeling of moral duty. We had been together for three-and-a-half years; not marrying would mean I had been playing with her and she had been wasting her time.

The morning of the religious wedding, I climbed a mountain and asked for a symbol for our marriage. I closed my eyes and saw two points of energy converging in descending flight, both moving together for awhile, then splitting with a sudden explosion. I didn't want to accept that so I asked for another symbol; this time it had to be physical. The mountain I was on had three very clearly defined levels; I was on its highest level when I asked to see a physical symbol for our marriage as the first object my eyes focused on at the lower level.

I went to the cliff and looked below. I saw a beggar; two dogs were following him. He was a nearly perfect representation of the Fool in the Tarot cards, the symbol of eternal change and supreme detachment. The beggar looked at me and greeted me with a smile. I started crying.

I had been forcing myself to believe all those years that the eagle's warning about its return in seven years, the experiences on the mountain, and the transits of Saturn and Uranus over my astrological Seventh House were only indications of disruptive forces I might be able to control if I really applied myself to being a decent husband. I had been looking for ways to escape my fate years in advance.

I even told my wife about my worries: "According to astrology, it seems that in four years I will have a career change and will withdraw for awhile. I would like for us to make a promise now that we will do our best to keep together during those difficult times."

She answered, "If you are afraid of the future you will call those problems to you. I don't want to make promises because I do not know what my frame of mind will be then, and because I do not want to bring trouble to our lives by believing it will happen."

Her strategy to cope with change didn't work.

I was working as a graphic designer, doing computer art in San Francisco when the inner pressure to stop following the establishment guidelines broke free. I decided to return to México and become a teacher of metaphysics full time. She became scared of the financial uncertainty of my new profession since it was my full responsibility to feed the family. She formally made me choose between the love and company of my family or my "juvenile dreams" that could cause me to be alienated and schizophrenic. She allowed me two weeks to make the decision. I chose, and lost all that I had, even my confidence in myself. Months later she would make every attempt, all futile, to get me to go back to her.

At that time I was studying a system of angelic magic, reputedly dangerous. I checked my potential success with it and was in a perfect position to undertake those invocations. I had nothing to lose because I had nothing left. The eagle had taken away my family, friends, fortune, and dreams; only my mind was left. Yes, I could lose my mind, but that was little risk compared to the possibility of recovering direct contact with the transpersonal levels of consciousness.

I traveled to northeast México to make a magical retreat in a cabin located on a ranch that had known better times and was now deserted. For fifteen days I invoked one by one the thirty Æthers of the Enochian system of angelic magic. I called the angels who supervise the dimensions existing between the physical level of reality and divine consciousness to guide and prepare me for my life's next stage.

Twice a day I put on a white robe. Standing in front of an improvised altar in the center of the room, I invoked the beings of light by means of a special magical language. This magical language temporarily liberated my mind from its interpretive function, allowing me to perceive streams of psychic events that were non-directed. These psychic allegories revealed my relationship with the spiritual worlds.

I underwent a most-profound transformation. A full alignment of my psychic levels took place during those days. Some of the Æthers were horrendous, some of them sublime. I was hearing angelic choirs every day, even on my ordinary levels of consciousness. The beings of those levels helped me to become a single-purposed individual again. Then I recorded my visions; here I include what I registered clairvoyantly and clairaudiently the last three days of my retreat:

> Third Enochian Æther—7/27/1987 8-9 pm
>
> Just before starting the ritualistic work I had an emotional outburst of thankfulness to God for each of the events of my existence. I relived my life's most-painful as well as its most-pleasant experiences. All looked to me as a marvelous symphonic unfolding of my consciousness, without a single discordant note.
>
> I came to realize that the First Commandment from the Tables of Moses was my first nature. In this upsurge of

THE HEART OF THE SERPENT

thankfulness and love, I felt all my being exploding toward the essence of divinity.

After performing the ritual I could see Hermes Trismegistus, the Greco-Egyptian god of wisdom and High Initiation for the alchemists and magicians of the past, inside the gazing stone, crowned, with an open book in his right hand. In his left hand he has the caduceus. He's stepping over another open book. Naked, floating in the universe, he says: "The knowledge of me is the knowledge of magic. Brother of Hermes, you are part of the chain of initiates since the beginning of time. You have come as a link from life to life, preparing the coming of the Christ force for the planet, opening the minds, extending the light, teaching what institutions don't teach. You have been with me since the beginning. You belong to my central sphere, to my intimate nucleus. From me you have come out to spread the light to the cosmos. Yes, my brother, you are another me. You are my incarnation on the planet, the incarnation of wisdom and peace. I love you. I love you as you love God, with all my being and all my strength. And all my essence showers over you. You are now, and always, the perfect representative of hermeticism on earth."

"Put my name on high. Your wisdom comes since the time of Melchizedek, and beyond him. You are the holy knight of the order of Melchizedek. Now I crown you with laurels. You have come to me again."

I have a vision of myself stepping up on a dais with seven steps. Each step has a symbol of a planet engraved on it. He is above the highest one. When I get to him, I kneel. And he puts a crown of laurel on me, and then his caduceus over my right shoulder. He says: "Stand up, son of Hermes. Now you and I are one."

I stand up and I hug him. And when I hug him, his subtle essence comes to me in the most exquisite fragrance. The most-pure essence that I have ever felt, crystalline, the perfect peace in the center of light. I want to stay in this state forever.

When I come again to focus my consciousness, I am looking from his perspective. I am Hermes Trismegistus. Opening my feet and legs in the position of the man of daVinci, I have wings on my heels, wrists, and temples, and a crown of gold over my head.

A pentagram is formed inside the circle. Both figures are luminescent, and they are superimposed over me like the geometrical figures that Vitruvius included in his medieval engraving of the microcosmos. I am in the perfection of divine geometry.

Then I see a great form coming toward me. It resembles a sphere, but when I look at it closely, it is composed of many facets, each a hollow, iridescent, protruding prism. Looking inside each prism, I can see the vacuous interior of the whole form. The prisms have precise hexagonal and pentagonal shapes, but at the same time the whole solid looks organic in form.

In my vision the majestic form comes over my head. It is about five times bigger than I am. I'm still in the likeness of Hermes, inside the pentagram and the circle. The geometric figure over my head radiates a resonant voice: "I am the universal consciousness, the memory bank of enlightenment that has been before you. Other sons and daughters of Hermes have been before. Ascend to me!" Flying up I come inside the geometric form through one of the prisms. All the prisms are transparent, but the edges of the facets glow with iridescent colors. The interior resembles an organic sponge. I feel in communion with the great minds of all times. Then I see Thoth, the Egyptian god of wisdom, in front of me. I hear him telling me, "Call to me below the skies at night during full moons. I'll come to you and I will enfold you, and I will give you what you need. Invoke me always in your heart." He disappears and then an Indian chief with a headdress and eagle feathers appears to me and says, "Son of Earth, anything you want will be given to you." Then I come down from the inside of the wondrous group mind. It emanates multiple electrical filaments coming to my body. With this I realize that my consciousness is indeed part of hermetic consciousness, and I have access to hermetic consciousness anytime I need. I can obtain all the hermetical knowledge I need through this group mind represented by the geometrical shape. A voice shakes in the Æther: "Son of Hermes, you are a master of Hermeticism. The sons of Hermes are known by their mental and intellectual development, and the use they give to it in the building of bridges for humanity to climb to higher consciousness."

A long time goes by, and then I have the vision of Venus emerging from the sea as in Botticelli's painting. But here everything is three dimensional. She's coming toward me in a big shell pulled by two dolphins. When she comes to the shore, she tells me: "Beauty and Love be in your life. I have been prisoner a long time in the dungeons of father Cronus. But now I have come to the light. It is time for me to live and to marry you." I open my arms in a cross. She comes and hugs me and she dissolves inside me, and then I hear, "Love and harmony are given to you."

Then I see a tree with a human face. His branches extend to heaven, and the countenance in the tree speaks to me: "I am the Tree of the Universe, the Tree of Life; the origin from which hermetic consciousness springs. In the nests between my branches the philosophers and magicians find their dwelling place. My limbs produce delicious fruits. I am the Tree of Good and Evil. My fruits took Adam out of Paradise, but now he comes in full consciousness. You are Adam, returning. Come to my limbs, to Paradise. To the Tree of Knowledge. Become intoxicated with my fruits because a little wisdom takes us away from God and more wisdom brings us back to Him."

I take a red apple and eat it. I can taste its exquisite flavor. And then I see the Eternal Father above my head. He smiles and speaks:

"This is the Tree of Good and Evil. Your tree. Take care of it. Protect it. Give its fruits to mankind so that they may return them to the Father. Each one at his own pace." And I understand clearly that for some people I will be Satan, and for others I will be Prometheus. I hear the voice of the Father in the Æther: "My son, the links in the chain first appeared when Atlantean wisdom was planted in the land of Kem [Egypt]. There we gather a compact body of knowledge, a group mind that will live forever. You are a projection of that group mind. You have been born to bring that essence to earth once more; that's your function. You should create hospices for the orphans of the Eternal Father. Teach them the sacred word, conduct them to light. How? You choose the way. There is nothing that can stop you. Your ordeals are over. You are the crowned alchemical Mercury."

Now, when I come to my body, I see in the gazing crystal Hermes closing a veil, a white veil, closing the vision in the crystal.

Second Æther—July 28, 1987   8:00-9:30 am

I see an incredibly beautiful young girl inside the gazing stone. She has a crown of flowers. She's naked, around fourteen-years old. She's throwing flowers and doves up into the air as she dances in happiness. I get inside the crystal and find myself very small at her side. She is about ten times larger than I am. All her body radiates a precious light-amber color. Her hair is in golden ringlets. Lirium flowers appear around her. It is an exquisite vision. I kneel before her and she starts to sing: "I am the universe in absolute perfection. I am the woman of the Tarot, the Twenty-First Arcana, the one that comes at the beginning and the end." Then I see a night sky that unveils; I get behind the veil; I am losing myself in ecstasy. Behind the veil there is a sanctuary that I shouldn't describe... It is the body of the naked Isis... I don't describe it because it is indescribable. There are no words; there is no mind that may conceive it or understand it. Only the total giving of the self. The knowing of how to be by not being...I am in a state of fusion... Or better, I am not.

Later I see the girl playing with a big lion. She challenges the lion to chase her, then laughs in ecstasy when it runs behind her. She now resembles an eight-year old. Her effervescent and crystalline laughter keeps me in a state of dissolution. She throws roses and other flowers to the lion. And the lion is playing with her. This symbolism involves Arcanum 11 of the Tarot cards. It is a pity that I cannot allow myself to drown completely in the vision. (If I do, I will not be able to relay my experience into the tape recorder.)

Now the girl looks immense, reaching to the sky. She's the real virgin, although she remains naked. After some time, I get close to a veil that covers another sanctuary. I remove the white curtain and from the back of the sanctum; over the altar that is inside it, an immense serpent springs over me. It has the head of a lion. In a moment the monster has grabbed my head and is eating me, and strangely, this produces in me another superior ecstasy. I am dissolving again, and this time I am becoming pure force, pure will.

After a long, long time I see the form of a Vesica Pisces. I have been transformed into a winged lion, with the body of a serpent. My body is emerald green. The scales on my front are orange amber. My mane is golden, my wings transparent like those of a dragonfly. The Vesica Pisces symbol keeps standing in front of me. In my new body I let myself be drawn into it. I don't know anything else about myself. I'm united. I'm united. I'm united. I have been unified. I have been unified. I have been unified. I have stopped to exist for the world. A very long time goes by. My physical body has spasmodic movements, and short and irregular breathing. I hear the words, "The last obstacle has been removed." And then I abandon myself completely to the forces of the Æther.

Again, many minutes elapse, then I hear the words, "He who loses his life for me will find it again." And then I speak with words that are not entirely mine: "I am the Son of my Father. I have been crucified and reborn again. I am what I am." A longer time goes by, and then I hear some voices that instruct me as to my purpose and my mission. They end by telling me, "You are consecrated as a master in full power."

First Æther—July 29, 1987 5:30-6:30 am

Inside the gazing crystal there is a little bearded child. He has a circle of light over his head. Behind him I see the figure of an old man, a hermit, who is being dissolved. Something tells me that I'm not there, that I'm not in any place. I see a magnificent green hawk regulating the universe. He looks like the god of Justice and Love, ruling in peace. Now he is on his throne, and I can see him frontally.

A long time elapses. I am nothing. I am not nothing. I am not everything. I am not myself. I hear the voice of an angel that tells me, "I have brought you pure and without stain to immolate you to the Lord." I throw myself over a sacrificial stone in front of me. My head is opened longitudinally by an angel's sword and my blood runs freely over the altar. A hexagram is formed over my head. I am dying, I am dying in the Lord.

The mind tries to reach high enough, the man tries to reach high enough, but it's impossible to get there from below. But the grace of the Lord is all. And it comes by itself when it wants. And it gets in, and nullifies and extinguishes what it finds. And becomes everything. In this way the manifestation of the Lord is immaculate.

Later I hear the chorus of the last movement of the Ninth Symphony of Beethoven, then a voice tells me: "Come, come back as much as you want, my son. This is your house. This is the dwelling from which no one has ever departed."

I see a bright serpent rising ecstatically in my vertebral column. There is nothing else. All of us are one. And my voice moves by itself, moved by the grace of the Lord: "Men will come before and after you. But the power, the force of your love will stay. You are seed from my tree, limb of my own, fruit of my own womb. I am that what I am, and you are inside me. And all that you do is perfect because you are mine forever. And all that you say is perfect because you belong to me forever. And each one of your manifestations is sacred because you are one with me forever. I speak through you, and you are my body on earth. And you are my love in the soul. And you are my blood that is reproduced between mankind. My beloved son, an eternal embrace. . ." Many minutes go by in full ecstasy. I am one with Him.

After a long time, I see a great dragon in intense white, very pure and iridescent in the sky over my head. And again, I submerge in *samadhi*, Oneness with All.

The voice comes again, "Go to do your will between men because I have given you carte blanche." Then I see an elegant, sinuous luminosity along my spinal column. It goes out of my head about eighteen inches and ends in a bright star. A long period of time goes by again. Then, from the depths of myself, the words come. "Father, what else do I need?" The Æthers reverberate with the words: "Nothing, my son. Nothing." And I lose myself again in divine consciousness.

At this point I come to realize that there has been almost no vision in this Æther. I try to get the crystal and put it to my brow to activate the visions, but I hear a clear voice that tells me, "Don't do it, son. The vision of the stone is a curse."

Again, a long time in perfect union. When I open my eyes everything is sanctified around myself. Outside there is a most-beautiful dawn, and the colors are saturated, seductive. I walk in the temple without the need to watch the dawn outside. Everything is perfect. I lie down without having closed the ritual. I am about to swoon. After ten minutes in bed, an absolute certainty that I live in every cell of my body assaults me. I am God.

After this magical retreat, it was time to return to my old life and prove I had faith in my revelations, even against any criticism from law, science, and religion.

My wife called me back home. The children were in great need of me, she said, so it was mandatory to make an extra effort. I thought she was right, but I had not realized yet how much the visions had changed me. I was not the same anymore. In less than two months away from home I had been renewed; my love was now directed to life. She was already a shadow in my past.

I went back for the children, but now my family life had the texture of dry sand. When I told her this time I wanted to leave to be on my own, she did all she could to stop me. I felt sincere pity for the woman who—at the time I decided to teach metaphysics—had thrown all my belongings outside our house, yelling that she needed a real man with her. Now she was calling our children, lawyers, priests, and psychologists on her behalf to stop me from leaving.

It turned into a big mess. First, I had to do battle with the ecclesiastical ideology of the most-respected religious figure in our city after the bishop—a monsignor who had been my teacher of Greek in previous years. This poor man was invited to dinner on three separate occasions to save my soul from the mortal sin I was about to commit. We discussed the dangers of divorce and of magic. Beyond his clergical functions, the man possessed a bright mind—he knew 21 languages, and was familiar with many Gnostic and Neoplatonic authors in whom I was interested in those days. The subject of angelic magic fascinated him. Between his official ecclesiastical admonitions he found enough time to ask sincere questions about my findings on magic, and he even asked to participate in one of my rituals!

The battle with the psychologists was more dangerous. They were my wife's ex-teachers and friends. She begged me to go to "marriage counseling," so we went to their sordid office on two occasions. Nobody would call what they did marriage counseling! At first they tried to pull my emotional cords to set me into the well-known sequence: closed-angry-tired-reconciled. When they saw they were not getting anywhere with me, they tried to persuade me in a most unprofessional way that going into divorce/metaphysics/magic was equal to fantasy/alienation/schizophrenia. They tried to scare me, and they did.

It took me two days to recover from their assault. The next week I was fine, and when they asked me: "Have you thought about what we have said? What is your opinion now?" Looking them straight in the eyes, I answered: "I really thought about what you said for a long time. I worried a lot about losing my mind if I take the path of divorce...but then I asked my magical mirror about all this, and it assured me I am not going crazy. So I don't worry anymore." They looked at each other and shrugged their shoulders. I was a lost cause for them. But I knew inside I had graduated that day to a new level of self-reliance.

When my wife saw she could not keep me any other way, she went to court and accused me of as many faults and aberrations as she could possibly imagine to keep full control over visits to my children and to use them as bait. Among other things, she accused me of intending to steal my own son to indoctrinate him in my dubious arts. Whenever I asked for guidance regarding my responsibilities to my children I saw images of Lot escaping from Sodom and Gomorrah. Looking back would mean becoming a salt statue. I had to move ahead or I would be frozen forever.

Following this inner feeling, I never appeared in court. I hired a lawyer and played my defense half-heartedly. I alternated between periods of indignation and rage at "what was being done to me" and periods of calm lucidity where I was able to see the archetypal dynamics of the crucifixion being enacted in modern times. Losing my children has been the most painful experience I have ever had, but when all this was over, my path became clear to pursue my mission.

5

THE PATHS THAT MADE MY PATH

From the age of three I remember feeling I had a mission in this life. I remember at the age of eight delighting in drawing balls of fire falling from heaven. At eleven I decided to reach the highest goal for a human being: initiating my studies in astrology, Oriental philosophy, alchemy, and phenomena beyond rational explanation. At sixteen I became part of a Yoga Institute in México City, learning astrology and yoga. I pursued my career in Graphic Design parallel to my esoteric studies. At seventeen, I became a teacher of astrology and Hatha yoga.

Around seventeen I discovered that my full name could be anagrammatized. My family name, "De La Lama," was already intriguing and is very close phonetically to "Dalai Lama." My friends at school used to make fun of me because of this similarity. One day by permutation of the letters of my first and family names, I constructed sentences in Spanish, which, when translated to English meant: "I know about the thunderbolt and its flame" and "Royal Sun of Light and Flame." Then my sense of mission was reinforced.

I had an eclectic training. I studied with many teachers, receiving initiations from Tibetan lamas, Hindu gurus, and magicians of German and Russian descent. I walked along different paths of yoga and obtained initiations and diplomas from several esoteric institutions. I studied diverse branches of psychology, feeling at home with the works of Jung and the transpersonal school.

While others were often blissfully falling into the auras of gurus all around, I often wondered why I could never make such a connection. All my spiritual relationships with earth-plane teachers had been temporary. Many times I felt strange and lonely, but in the back of my mind I always knew that everything was only a preparation for my mission.

In 1981 I reached the apex of my yearning for the discovery and actualization of my mission. For years I had been obsessed with the possibility of communicating with my Guardian Angel. The Kabalistic and other esoteric traditions say that once the contact with the Guardian Angel is established, he provides all the information needed for the rest of the spiritual journey, as well as the part you are supposed to play in the cosmic scheme. Imagine this: An invisible master with all the wisdom you need, always present, devoted to your well-being and spiritual growth. What else could you ask from life? I didn't care if it were a part of me or a lofty being of the higher dimensions. The actualization of this possibility was a passion that absorbed my thoughts for a long time.

There was another reason for my fixation on the Guardian Angel, that is, a conscious dream occurring in 1979 in which I came to a simple but beautiful golden shrine with an aura of purity and righteousness. There was a dais with three steps and over it a rectangular altar like those seen in churches; it had a sword and a cup on it. Behind the altar a solar angel was standing. He was dressed in orange-yellow and a full-sized ruby-red Calvary cross ornamented his robe's front. His hair was golden and his eyes full of purpose. He was waiting for me. I didn't dare climb the stairs but walked as close to him as possible, and then I knelt. He grabbed me by my arms. His grip was strong, commanding. He forced me to ascend the stairs and stand in front of him, saying: "You shouldn't kneel. I bless you for you to be like me."

I studied old magical grimories that offered obscure instructions on how to attain this angelic contact and worked at the rituals with all my heart. During one of these magical operations, often followed by prolonged meditations, I came to realize that what seemed to be my great and noble aspiration was just a way to satisfy the need for guidance and closeness I had never had with my father. When this insight appeared in my meditation I said to myself: "Look at you, Luis, still looking for a Daddy!" I felt ashamed. I felt stupid. But I could not shake the desire to contact my Guardian Angel even when I recognized it was coming from a psychological dysfunction!

I persevered like a rabid dog in my pursuit until a conscious dream let me know the futility of it all. In the dream a wise old man extended a parchment roll for me to read. It clearly said the Guardian Angel would not come to me because I was unable to enjoy life as a normal human being. With my obsession for achievement I was ungrateful for what life was offering me at that time.

I envisioned my life's strategy as simple as this: Try to talk with the Guardian Angel and then do what he says. That's it. However, experience taught me true spiritual growth is not that simple.

It was on May 12, 1986, when living in San Francisco, that I finally made a steady contact with the Guardian Angel—or rather, he disclosed himself to me. For about a year I had been practicing a special meditation technique, that is, daily visualizing a medieval castle. Each room of this castle was a symbol for a specific level of consciousness that allowed me to attune with a particular archetypal frequency in the universe. In the different rooms I related to beings who were dynamic representations of the powers of each plane of awareness.

There was a chapel in this castle representing the perfect center of harmony and beauty in the universe. It happened that in my midnight meditation when I approached the chapel to make the daily offering of myself to the evolutionary forces, the narrow corridor to the chapel was blazing with golden light. As I approached it I could clearly and strongly feel golden dust in my eyes. The angel whose aura emanated this light was in the chapel. He told me his name and confirmed he was my Guardian Angel.

His message was very different from anything I had expected. He said my mission was to find my own strategies to bring my spiritual essence to earth and to take full responsibility for my actions. No detailed information was necessary for me since I was about to become a leader, not a follower. The beings on the spiritual planes were preparing me to become one of them—a Master, not a disciple.

My angel was kind enough to let me know the essentials: I had come to earth to manifest the powers of the sun under the procedures of the purple ray of ceremonial order and magic.

Those days I used to test the truthfulness of my visions by means of *gematria*, esoteric numerology, or a branch of Kabalistic knowledge more complex than ordinary Pythagorean numerology. I checked the name of the angel using this procedure, and its correlations with the orthodox esoteric body of knowledge were good enough to satisfy me. But the real test came when in the next few days I found a book called *A Dictionary of Angels* by

Gustav Davidson. There I found the name of my angel, a name that sounded rather plain and even funny to me because of the close phonetic association with an ordinary Spanish word, which in Hebrew stands for a very holy being. It is the name of the angel of the Merkabah, the holy chariot that took Elias and Ezekiel to heaven.

Another spiritual being, however, was more interested in working with me. The first sign of his presence came a few months after the shocking experience with Carlos Castaneda's gift. It was 1:00 am and I was driving back from a full-moon meditation with a sixty-year-old magician. This was the second time we had met and the first time we meditated together. My first impression of her was that of an old woman with little theoretical background relating to our mutual interests. At our first meeting she didn't like the fact that I liked Aleister Crowley's books, and she made that known to my friends immediately. She was concerned about the purity of my aims and suspicious about anything coming from me. We changed our views about each other that night.

At the end of the meditation she told me in front of the group: "I didn't recognize you at first. Now I know who you are. You were in the highest chambers of Initiation with me and it was your mission to teach others. In my vision tonight you were extending papyrus rolls to those in the lower degrees, then you were to sit naked on a purple throne that, more than a throne, was a flame. You were inside the flame and a powerful voice said: 'Your name is Anú.'"

Her praise didn't make too much sense to me then, but there on the road I suddenly intuited the meaning of the name. I was very fond of Egyptian mythology then. I said aloud, "Of course! 'Anú' means 'Anubis!'" And exactly at the same time, appearing from nowhere, my car was surrounded by four dogs running playfully at the same speed I was driving since the road was badly damaged. They all resembled Anubis, the Egyptian god of magic whose function is the conductor of souls through the gates of the other world. His other name is "The Opener of the Ways."

I could not believe my eyes. It was not an hallucination, but a perfect synchrony with my thought, or perhaps even a materialization. The dogs never barked. It was a silent display of protection and friendship. Then they stopped, but when I tried to locate them in the mirror, they were gone. I drove around the block to look at them once more, but I could not find them.

The old magician became a great partner for many magical operations since that night. She is very powerful. Her will never wavers. We aimed at very precise results in the financial and political worlds and the effects of our work were clear. She is the finest magician I have ever worked with.

Anubis kept coming in my meditations; he appeared in my astral castle often to teach me new magical procedures. He was instrumental in my encounter with my Twin Soul, the most-wonderful event that helped actualize my mission.

My clairvoyant abilities slowly developed over many years of daily spiritual discipline; I also succeeded in reaching at will several stages of cosmic consciousness. In 1985 I met with two Hindu gurus, heads of their respective organizations, and the Dudjom Rinpoche, the Supreme Head of one of the four lines of Tibetan Buddhism, second only to the Dalai Lama. I asked them on separate occasions what my next spiritual accomplishment in meditation should be. After I described my experiences in the higher realms of consciousness, they all said that I needed no more directions, but should follow my own intuition.

Somehow I felt disappointed. The books spoke of cosmic consciousness as the end of the Great Work. You become reintegrated with the universal mind. You go back to God. It is said that this state of consciousness shatters all preconceived notions of reality and makes you a kind of spiritual hero. I knew I had achieved that state several times, but the results were not as impressive as I thought they would be. After sublime states of meditation I would be the same ordinary person, with my same apprehensions and problems. "Where are those spiritual rewards they speak of?" I thought again and again. Slowly I discovered a shocking cultural difference as the reason for the illusion under which I had been laboring.

Eastern cultures had been built around the value of spiritual achievement as the highest desirable good. Just as in the West you see a T.V. commercial persuading you that by buying the latest car model you will achieve lasting fulfillment, in the East gurus and monks exaggerate the results of enlightenment. Yes, if you meditate for ten or fifteen years you, too, can begin to feel you don't need a body to exist, you can feel your consciousness encompass the totality of space, that you breathe with the rhythms of the stars, that you are a crystal clear transmitter of the will of God, a Messiah for the lower worlds of manifestation. Meditations of this kind soothe you, help you to control stress, but after these wonderful subjective experiences, you will be the same old you. Yet no miraculous transformations occur at this stage.

In fact, you are closer to trouble than ever because it is easy to fall into the trap of spiritual pride and believe that "Your kingdom is not of this world." Your consciousness then splits into the longing for more of those supremely subjective joys of the higher worlds and a dislike for the rest of the time spent attending to basic survival needs.

The earth then becomes a hell. Once you taste the sweet temptations of heaven in your meditations, your job, taking care of the kids, doing housework all become different forms of torture. I know many New Age practitioners struggling with this duality: what they reject the most becomes their shadow. When they would rather be meditating day and night in some kind of spiritual commune, they are forced to deal with crisis after crisis. This is the way their shadow forces them to realize that in addition to their infinite selves they think they have reached, they are also the darkness of the world they reject.

I learned from experience that enlightenment comes like the waves of the ocean. At first the grace of the Spirit descends upon you and you have no control over its visitations. When this happens at an early age it colors the direction of your life. Without sufficient intellectual ability to understand these phenomena, you could become a fanatic, or someone who thinks God has spoken to him/her and now has the key to all the riddles of the universe.

At this stage you may frequently think that if you "meditate" diligently enough on the memories of enlightenment, you can bring them back to life. This is like trying to rekindle the fire of the mystical experience by bringing a match close to the ashes. It never works.

It takes some time to realize that the best way to move closer to enlightenment is by living in the present, and to work on the removal of the obstructions that individualized consciousness presents to expanded awareness. You must pierce the veils by focusing the torch of awareness on them—not by trying to guess what is on the other side.

The process of enlightenment is perplexing because you often think you have secured levels of awareness that later will be lost in the continuous dissolutions and syntheses of your consciousness. The great French magician, Eliphas Levy, so accurately described the whole process of materialization in his drawing of Baphomet, the obscure god that templar knights supposedly worshipped in secret. Baphomet represents the world of substance and the illusions that affix the consciousness to it. He also represents the shadow of those desiring to escape the physical world. Although Levy depicted Baphomet as the devil, Baphomet is, nonetheless, the master of material existence. And all of those who desier to materialize their dreams will have to deal with him sooner or later.

Anubis many times visited the castle I built in my meditations. Merlin was there at times also teaching me exercises in the use of the energy from my hands later to be instrumental in my present work.

By now I had quit my career as a graphic designer to become a full-time metaphysical counselor and teacher. I trained people in Meditation, Yoga, Astrology, Reincarnation Psychotherapy, Bio-magnetic Healing, Clairvoyance, Mystical Kabalah, Tarot Symbolism, Angelic Contacts, and several other subjects. I became a professional magnetic healer in México, and this without any advertisement on my part. My students referred their friends and relatives to me, and eventually I was working three days a week using biomagnetic energies up to eleven hours daily without depletion! I found that I was working as a continuous transformer of cosmic powers, and not as a rechargeable battery; the more I used the energy, the stronger I became. My psychic abilities increased and, at the end of every day dedicated to healing, the higher energy always made me feel bathed in bliss.

From time to time I came across patients with very heavy negative energy and realized that these people had been cursed by Mexican witches or sorcerers. Most psychic healers find these cases extremely difficult to deal with because the negative energies are sticky and can transfer themselves to the aura and the environment of the healer. In my case nothing like this ever happened; my work area became increasingly charged with positive energy. Patients and friends noticed the purity in the room as they entered.

On only one occasion was I forced to reflect the black-magic energy to its sender. One of my students those days was a Ph.D. in psychology, former director of the psychology department of the most prestigious university in México City. She looked for my help in healing a high-society lady who was involved in politics. Her patient had thyroid gland and skin problems, as well as sudden asphyxia attacks seemingly of psychosomatic origin. After several ineffective sessions with her, my student intuited that something else was preventing the healing.

Her patient, wearing a long red-satin skirt and more gold jewelry than necessary, was a beautiful woman of about 40 years. As she entered the room I told her I was seeing a dark fog around her legs, especially the left one. She pulled her skirt up to let me see the purple spots all over her skin. "I have been with many Mexican and American dermatologists and nobody knows what is going on with me," she said. "Do you know what this is all about?" I followed the etheric lines of energy with my clairvoyant vision to their source. I saw a woman doing a spell with the patient's pantyhose. The man who provided the pantyhose for the woman to cast the spell was trying to keep the rich woman in love with him.

When I told her what I saw, she then confirmed she was living with a man who was ruining her relationship with her daughters, that she was "very generous" with this man, and that he was a professor who had studied several books about magic. And... that she remembered losing a pair of her pantyhose in the past.

At the time of clearing the etheric links and grounding the negative energy, I perceived an evil creature imbedded in my patient's heart. I had never seen anything like it before. I tried to extract it magnetically with my hands, but it resisted with the stubbornness of a bear. When I succeeded in moving the creature out of place, it would jump back to its place as soon as I removed the psychic tension. It took me twenty-five minutes to disintegrate the psychic parasite! The woman became really amazed since she was now able to breathe freely. But most important was her change of attitude about the man. Suddenly she stopped feeling attracted to him. She decided at that moment to break off the relationship and to ask him to leave her house. I recommended that she not talk to the professor about our meeting.

Four days later I returned from a short trip to Los Angeles. My psychologist friend had been calling me on the phone insistently. When I reached her she was in tears. She had been feeling the devil around her! She could not describe her impressions any other way. She told me the devil was trying to take possession of her heart, that from her clinical perspective she thought she was going mad, but from the esoteric perspective something horrid kept continuously trying to control her. Day and night she had to pray to keep an invisible demon in abeyance.

As my psychologist friend lived three hours from my house, I offered long-distance healing, gave her a few recommendations, then asked her to call our mutual patient to find out if she had mentioned anything to the professor. Our patient told her that, although she had not said anything about me, she explained to her lover that she had been in counseling and was thinking seriously about breaking up. The man had then asked her every detail concerning the therapy, the name of the therapist, and had finished the conversation by telling her that she should not make such a drastic decision because she was very stressed out. He then said he knew she would soon be much better and would see things differently.

After three absentee healing sessions to help my friend, and after finding out my work was only effective for an hour or two, I did an Egyptian ritual to turn back the evil onto the sender. I was informed two weeks later that the professor (a man of no more that 45 years) suffered a sudden heart attack and had to be sent to México City for open-heart surgery.

I had several other wild experiences with sorcery, but it would be in bad taste to fill several pages with eerie stories involving an area of the invisible worlds better left alone. I have battled the "Holy Death," a spirit of ancient prehispanic sorcery, filtered in our times through semi-Christian prayers, sent to kill one of my patients by her husband's mistress. At another time I had to disintegrate the etheric body of a prisoner spirit, that of a dead Amazonian Indian, possibly of the Jíbaro tribe, appointed as guardian of the belongings of a powerful shaman who was living in the city. The prisoner spirit was avenging the intrusion of a charming lady who had gone into the shaman's apartment and touched his power objects out of curiosity when he was not there.

That night her intestines became paralyzed and the woman had to have ten-inch exploratory surgery, but the doctors could not find any organic problem. She almost died before I could do something about it.

One day I was invited to a demonstration of an energy system in Los Angeles. The founder, my friend had told me, although he resembled a moron, had a very powerful aura, and was using theosophical cosmology as a basis for his work. I was familiar with theosophy as well as with Alice Bailey's writings, her additions and clarifications almost as deep and abstruse as the inspired works of Helena Petrova Blavatsky. This energy system piqued my curiosity.

The founder of the system was as inarticulate in his speech as he was awkward of body, but nobody could deny his energy. When one of his students put her hands over me I saw a blue angel with a crown of gold. This being took me to a golden city (Shambhala) where old people asked me if I was willing to help them anchor spiritual energies on our planet. I accepted and immediately I was brought back to my body—all this happening in about two minutes.

Although I was not strongly impressed by this vision, I still thought its meaning clearly indicated that I should pursue training with the strange group. It wasn't until months later that the full meaning of the words of the Masters of Shambhala became evident to me.

In less than a year I became a teacher of this energy system. But I saw it was not doing any good for the personalities involved. Every teacher was caught up in power trips, most of the meetings were spent telling low-grade jokes, always with a sexual content. The founder stated that he was the reincarnation of Annie Besant, a famous second-generation theosophist, President of the organization. The vice-president of the organization used to give short "inspirational" speeches assuring everyone that this energy system would be the one to replace Christianity for the next two-thousand years! At some point the founder thought the organization's marketing strategies should be upgraded so he devised a new presentation package. The system then became the only one in the world to offer all the possible shaktis, or energies of creation according to Hindu cosmogony.

During that time I was being contacted telepathically by diverse deities and angelic beings. They were giving me the codes to call their energies at will. However, I made a mistake when I proudly demonstrated my new healing frequencies to him, and explained about their source. The founder stole the names and registered them, claiming he had received the new energies at the time of physical encounters with the mythical Invisible Masters of the Transhimalayan Hierarchy.

As my sensitivity opened up, my awareness of the beings of light increased, and their telepathic messages became clearer. They told me that I was about to receive a system to increase and develop human energy which would be based on the qualities of fire. This system would be compatible with any spiritual path and would be specially suited for the Western world.

Over a period of months many different angels appeared to me. It happened in the middle of my energy-healing sessions, during my meditations, rituals, and reveries while crossing the high mountains between Tijuana and Mexicali, a trip I used to take every week since most of my students lived in the state capital of Baja California.

Most of these angels gave me a set of codes to call their energies at will—any time I needed them. They all had different frequencies and their energies could be used for different purposes in healing. I tried them on my patients and they were always effective. My most-sensitive students were able to describe the effects of the energies just as I experienced them on the first visit of the angels.

A typical encounter with an angel generally happened in the following manner: It often occurred as I was relaxing after four or more hours of almost continuous healing work with my patients. My hands where clasped on the back of my head on the couch where I used to do healing work. The energy from my hands inadvertently activated my Third-eye chakra so that I entered into a kind of blissful state where I saw a sphere of light the size of a big building coming from the zenith directly over me until my physical body was encompassed in the center of the sphere. Then a soft voice spoke to me: "I am the angel of harmony. From now on you will not do healing work by replacing old, stagnant energy with fresh spiritual energy. It won't be a linear process anymore. This symbol will allow you to transform the lines of force of the negative energy field itself, and rearrange its inner geometry into a harmonious mandala. The same energy particles will align in this new formation and health will manifest soon."

In a similar way I was contacted by many beings of light from the Hindu, Egyptian, Greek, Enochian, Essenian, and Kabalistic traditions. These beings taught me the codes to call their power at will, and, through this, I learned to handle a wide spectrum of energies.

Since many of my students were psychologists and psychiatrists, I could speak their language and demonstrate what I talked about. Many times they referred patients to me they could not work with. Although I was respected and admired and had reached a new platform of stability, the inner fire was preparing another leap into the unknown.

There was another mysterious being that appeared at times in the castle of my meditations; I called him the eagle Master. I have never seen his face; maybe he doesn't have one, but on every occasion the contact is established I see an imperial double-headed eagle in my mind's eye. I think this eagle Master is somehow related to the wild energy I had to battle and then integrate after meeting Carlos Castaneda. My guess is that he was there from the beginning, supervising the whole process. It was only when I purified enough of myself that he began his telepathic transmissions.

On the winter solstice of 1987 I was meditating on top of La Rumorosa (The Whispering One), the Sierra dividing the Mediterranean weather areas of northern Baja from the inland desert. During the meditation I reached full expansion and perfect transparency: I was all there is. At that point I saw myself going into a mysterious mansion where the eagle Master was waiting for me. He asked me, "Are you prepared to leave all that you have achieved up to now? You are a cosmic being, a teacher for the world; I will take you to positions of power, but be prepared to leave your life as you know it."

I asked for physical proof that he had been there. I opened my eyes and a reflection of the sun hit them. It was coming from a small metal bottle cap on the ground, turned upside down. I reached out for it and upon turning it over I found it had an eagle painted on its top!

Soon after that my life changed dramatically. I was invited to demonstrate bio-magnetic energies at the United Nations. The night before flying to New York during my meditation, I saw an immense being made of living fire. He grabbed me as one would an insect, and in the next moment, opened his mouth and ate me. When I was inside him he talked to me: "You are part of me now. You are of my same essence. You will be my contact on earth to deliver my power to humanity."

I was shaken by the vision, but its meaning was not yet evident to me until three days later when I went to the Agni Yoga Museum in New York City. At the time of the vision I had no idea that I would be going to that museum, so it was a pleasant surprise to find paintings of the same being of my vision there. He was Agni, the God of Fire of Hindu mythology. This was synchronous proof that I was being contacted by a very high spiritual power.

On the third floor of this museum, I saw another painting showing the entrance of a cave between two rocks. The painting, entitled *Ashram*, opened another dimension to me as I stood in the middle of the exhibition room in front of it. I was fully aware of what was going on around me, but at the same time was inside the cave with Master Morya, a widely known member of the Transhimalayan Brotherhood. He was dressed in red and gave me an initiation of fire, repeating what Agni had said previously.

Almost a year later the god of fire and Master Morya would teach me a full system of practices and initiations to integrate the fiery spiritual essence into human beings—a path that would include techniques never taught before to purify imprints from previous lives that hold onto the unconscious mind and condition perception and experiences in this lifetime.

By strange synchrony, the exact day of my thirty-third birthday, at the same hour I was born, I gave the talk at the United Nations building. After the demonstration I felt another being coming into my telepathic awareness; it was something impressive, nothing less than the Planetary Ruler! He asked me to come again the next day and establish a link between the United Nations and the cosmic energies I had invoked in my private disciplines over the past few years.

The next morning I took a guided tour through the United Nations building. As we proceeded through the rooms I helped to empower the different meeting rooms with the universal ideal of brotherhood by calling down spiritual energy and angelic choirs to sustain the positive changes. With the power of my Third Eye, I built unifying bridges between the seats used by the diplomatic groups. Suddenly I was telepathically informed by one of the Invisible Masters in charge of the U.N. project that the whole U.N. territory was a gigantic talisman used to radiate to earth the main concepts of the philosophy of the New Era.

The tour completed, I asked permission to enter the meditation room which was at that time always locked. Whenever they opened it upon request, a guard was required to remain in the room with you, and you were allowed to stay for only three to five minutes. The first guard refused me access to the room. Yet I knew it was essential for me to get in because that same morning as I approached the U.N. building I had seen a gigantic vortex of cosmic energy concentrating on its top, with its upper part extending into outer space. It resembled an immense tornado, formed by an unthinkable amount of galactic spiritual essence, ready to make a link with our planet.

My intuition told me to ask one particular guard for permission to enter the meditation room. This man opened it for me, and then left the room, closing the door and forgetting all about me for the next 45 minutes—more than sufficient time needed to do my work.

The room was completely painted in blue, had a trapezoid floor plan, and was softly and indirectly lit. The only direct light source was a single, intense beam in the middle which shone on the center of a big rough semi-rectangular stone resembling a primitive altar. Once there I did a ceremony to link the cosmic energy to the altar-stone which, for my particular work, represented mankind. At some point, carried away in the magical activity, I placed seven of my fingers in a curious geometrical position over the altar and immediately felt the presence of the seven Masters of the Transhimalayan Brotherhood. The work was done. I saw the altar-stone pulsating with a new power of synthesis, becoming almost transparent with each pulsation.

Nobody was informed about the cosmic charge to the stone, but, nevertheless, in the next few days, a lady I know who leads a yoga group within the United Nations building told me that her group had a most strange impression when they meditated there after my visit. Being a well-known group, they were the only ones to have unsupervised access to the place. They found a new spiritual quality in the room's atmosphere and felt the stone at the center pulsating and becoming transparent from time to time, just as I perceived it at the end of my work.

The many paths that made my path converged after this magical operation. At the United Nations building meditation room I offered myself as a focal point for the distribution of cosmic energies to earth. After this event my destiny took a course of its own. I did not have to search anymore. Everything was given to me.

6

MY EXPERIENCE OF THE GODDESS

I love the Goddess with boundless passion. I want her like an animal, like a demon. My force field inflames at her very name.

I rend asunder my skull and pluck every thought as a sacrifice in her name. With my own bones I drum the original rhythm, calling her, echoing her waves while I sleep lucid dreams in the throbbing of her womb. I have offered my flesh in the cycles of becoming. I have laid my whole existence at her feet.

In her diaphanous luminescence I revel in pleasure; in her unbeheld depths I despair in yearning. There is a sweet torment in her mystery, in her continuous receding. It is the capricious game she has found to unshield my fierce will that now stands naked in immensity. And she comes from everywhere, kissing away the last edge of my boundaries, blowing apart the streams of my thought. She undoes me; she possesses me with unutterable lightness and I melt on the tip of her tongue.

Her aesthetic assails are more devastating than her unpredictability; she drowns me in beauty and enslaves me in indescribable rapture—and I always want more.

I am the man of her dreams because she is dreaming me, and in her dreaming me, I become. I do not fear extinction because I am not, and because she is night, and sleep, and prophecy. As a thought in her mind I can live forever, and change forever. As a creation of her fancy I can fold back into her in the end and become what I have always been.

I breathe her. She breathes me. I advance through fields of darkness feeling her, smelling her, penetrating deeper and deeper in her warmth. I conquer blazing mountains of sacred desire only to throw myself in the abyss of her body, universal void that dissolves might and merit, drive and aim. I am alone inside her perpetual unveiling simply to experience the joy of fusion. I am speed, roaming aimlessly in delight in the exhilaration of her eternal yielding to my advance. I am a supernova dying in ecstasy in her vault.

This is the story of our romance. The Goddess has come to me in many faces, gradually unveiling the omnipresence of her body in my life.

My story begins with a dream I had when I was four-years old. In this dream a green fairy lent me her magic wand, and I discovered I could produce a beam of stars with it, a starry beam that disintegrated everything it touched. I was on the stage of a theater, very excited about my toy, covering everything in sight with a beam of stars. Unfortunately, I overlooked the green fairy, and made her accidentally disappear in the torrent of my wand.

I spent the rest of the dream mourning for my benefactor, desperately searching for the green fairy, whom, I believed, had been transported somehow to another dimension I was unable to reach.

This is the first dream I remember. Over the years I have interpreted it in several ways, knowing it was one of the keys to the recovery of my wholeness. It reveals, among other things, the loss of conscious contact with the power of love and my feminine counterpart (green is the color of Venus, the planet of love and the feminine side of nature) because of my indiscriminate use of the direct, masculine approach (the phallic magic wand).

My main interest in life has always been magic and the high states of consciousness that are the goal of different spiritual disciplines. I was so involved in these fields I never gave enough attention to human relationships. I learned to love the feminine side of God in every aspect of nature, and although I sometimes longed for a physical woman, I felt quite happy with my almost ascetic life.

Many times in my magical training I heard the voice of the Goddess in meditation. This was always a shock to me, since during those days I thought of the Masters on the invisible planes as all male; I suffered from negative indoctrination on the subject of women and spirituality.

The esoteric order in which I did my first incursions in yoga and astrology deemed that women could not possibly go beyond the second initiatic degree, but men were always able to go to the seventh, which was the highest for this organization. The reason for this discrimination, as explained by the founder, was that women were unable to transcend their emotional natures.

Philosophically, the issue of discrimination was nauseating to me from the beginning, but there were few institutions offering a path to enlightenment in México those days. Eventually I forced myself to believe that those guys in their secret chambers of the higher degrees knew what they were doing, and accepted provisionally the discrimination. Until I learned more about the interrelations of physiology, psychology, and enlightenment, I would play by their rules and would disregard feminine energy as low and unreliable. Now I know better. It is by experience I have come to realize that for the male psyche the only chance for lasting integration of the spiritual perceptions is through the gate of the Goddess. Other experiences of enlightenment will always leave a residual memory of triumph and achievement: The hero has conquered darkness! This mode of perceptual enlightenment soon decays into spiritual pride since the hero cannot become one with that which he conquers. He is still on a pedestal—aloof and laureate. All this sets the stage for future defeat under the cycles of the immutable law of rhythm.

By the time I had resigned my position in that order I understood enough analytical psychology and Egyptian magic to accept the possibility of my feminine counterpart, or Goddess, as part of my magical universe. Yet I was, nevertheless, suspicious of her influence. The writings of Aleister Crowley helped model my understanding of the feminine during those days, with all his devotion and all his contempt, his sado-masochistic rapture, and his megalomaniacal statements.

I admire Crowley's work up to this day and owe him much. Unfortunately, it has become fashionable for bland, cowardly, hypocritical, illiterate New Agers to renounce him. I know some of my readers feel this way, largely because they have not read his works. And those who have read them and have not understood them will worry about his philosophical/spiritual contamination of my approach to enlightenment. I regard him as a great scholar and initiate of the first rank. He intuited and brought through the genius of his writing truths of a very deep order, truths about human nature psychology is just beginning to unravel today, truths inexorably becoming part of the social standards of our times.

Nevertheless, Crowley's imperfect vision of a perfectly unbounded spiritual love impossible to potentiate in a one-to-one relationship negatively colored my world until the experience of living with my Twin Soul made me understand the torments of Crowley's powerful and sensitive soul, alone without a match on this plane of existence.

Often I invoked Nu, the Egyptian goddess of the night sky, and Artemis, the virginal hunter goddess of the moon. Whenever I felt the Goddess around me I experienced bursts of unconditional love that didn't fit too well with the self-styled magician I was still trying to become: cold, detached, and in full dominion of the invisible worlds.

By the time I married for the first time—after the eagle experience—I was already very pliable, a condition perhaps as unbalanced as the past juvenile macho approach to the Mysteries. This made me yield to the negative spectrum of the feminine energies: oppression, stagnation, manipulation. Still deluded by Crowley's perspective of love (I did not know better those days) I surrendered to a life in which my mystic contacts with the Goddess were only in heaven; however, I accepted without question the negative side of Her spectrum in my everyday life.

When the subject of divorce came up between my wife and me, I felt waves of guilt for days. The whole issue made me go through a painfully introspective period. I was seriously concerned about creating a karmic debt with the Goddess if I failed to satisfy my wife. One afternoon I was meditating on all of this when Isis, the Egyptian goddess of the all-pervading feminine power, appeared in my mental field spontaneously, and said to me, "Have you thought about all the good things you can give to other women if you leave your present wife?" I had never thought of that before. Her words opened the road to freedom to me. Since then I found out that in my future work as an instructor of applied metaphysics most of my students were women!

It was one of those women who later became a temporary vessel for the Goddess, and the focus of a story that demonstrates the phenomenon of synchrony in its purest mathematical expression.

In Kabalah, 7 is one of the numbers of the Goddess—in this case Lady Venus, who operates through the 7th emanation of

God according to Kabalistic cosmology. The number 21, being 3 x 7, represents the descent of the Goddess to the three-fold world of creation; the 21st major card in the Tarot depicts the Goddess dancing in the center of the four basic elemental energies.

On July 25, 1987 (and please note that $1 + 9 + 8 + 7 = 25$, and $2 + 5 = 7$, and July is the 7th month, so we have three 7s in that date), I proceeded as usual in the discipline of the magical retreat I was pursuing in those days. I purified the interior of the log cabin in the woods where I was living alone for the extent of the retreat. I put on my white robe, took my consecrated wand in one hand, and my book of Enochian invocations in the other. I called the angels of the 7th æther to open up to me a vision of that subtle realm of consciousness.

At the time I was not conscious of the meaning of the date in regard to the symbolism of the number 7. My concentration on the 7th æther was coincidental since during the previous days I had been invoking other æthers, raising my consciousness from the 30th æther, the lower level of the mind, going up to the first level, the level of communication with God. At the end of the invocation, I turned on a tape recorder and described the visions and messages I was perceiving while gazing at a large clear quartz crystal in the center of an improvised altar with candles surrounding it. Therein I saw a great archangel in deep-blue robes, a feminine archangel, coming out of the sea. Immediately this archangel became the Goddess and spoke to me: "Look for a woman who is able to open up the whole of her soul. She should expand in love. I will give her to you. Her name is Christina. Twenty-one days. Love her and transform her into a diamond-woman. She will cross your path; she will come to you. You will recognize her." I transcribed this piece of information without a second thought. It formed part of a collection of seventy pages of single-spaced type written materials at the end of the retreat. All this went into a niche on my library shelves.

Twenty-one days after this vision was the time of the Harmonic Convergence. I met with friends and students and conducted a ritual for sixty people. After the activities were over, a woman came to me. Her name was Maria Elena. She told me that she was feeling a strong connection with me and asked if I could explain why. No thoughts of my Enochian experience were in my mind when I answered her: "Well, it may be that your higher self has noticed something in me that will be instrumental in your evolution. Perhaps this means that there is something we should do together." I invited her to do ritual.

Once a week in my Tijuana basement temple we invoked the Gods through ancient Egyptian magical formulas. She always carried the archetypal mother energy. Maria Elena's natural talent was phenomenal. Our magical interaction helped us remember past incarnations in Egypt, and I became clearly aware of my power and cosmic function at that time.

On November 5, 1987, I wrote this in my magical diary: "Last night I meditated at the beach. It was a beautiful clear night, with the full moon over the ocean. I saw beautiful ancient sculptures of winged cats and then, suddenly, I realized that the name "Maria Elena" had the same numeric value as the name "Christina." Two days ago, without knowing anything about my Enochian experiences, or about the significance of the number 7, she gave me a card that she signed with her self-chosen magical motto: 'Seventh Heaven.'"

Gematria is Kabalistic numerology, not the usual exoteric divination system based on numbers, but a way to understand the connection between everything in the universe by knowing the number that the letter's values in a word add up to, then establishing mathematical relationships between them. I had studied *gematria* in the early 80s, so that night I went to my books and found that, indeed, by gematric correspondences, both the names Christina and "Maria Elena" added up to 343, and that 343 is 7^3.

I became aware that the information was received from the 7th æther. And she, without knowing anything about this, had picked up the magical name "Seventh Heaven." She came to me 21 days (7 + 7 + 7) after the invocation to the 7th æther. Of course, Maria Elena was representing the Goddess all the time. Realization of this synchrony came to me under the influence of the full moon, another symbol of the Goddess.

It was due to our magical work together that the telepathic contact with the Goddess became stronger and stronger every day.

Then, in my meditations, the Goddess appeared to tell me she was coming in the flesh to my life. When? The time was not yet.

Maria Elena became a great friend; our relationship was always from the heart up. I remember a long, serious talk with her husband, a rich and sensitive man who was able to understand the spiritual needs of Maria Elena. He put those needs over his Mexican macho training—his jealousy and uncertainty. To this day I am as grateful to this man as I am to Maria Elena for the work that we were able to do together.

Living in Florida alone gave me an opportunity to restructure my relationship with the feminine. On September 10, 1988, I was in the middle of a sixteen-day sequence of invocations to the angels of the metaphysical elements, but my mind was not at ease; excessive celibacy was proving detrimental to my magical work. After the invocation I complained to the heavens about my condition; I ended my pleas in an angry mood, finishing the invocation with the words: "Bring me peace of mind or bring me a woman." Then I went into meditation, and later wrote in my magical diary:

> The visions were very realistic and eerie. I was in the Hall of Judgment of the Egyptian Underworld, Maat [The Egyptian goddess of Justice] put me on the scales of balance, and unlike many other times, when I have seen myself there, I was found impure. Then I saw Set

approaching me [the god of physical substance and time]. He took me down to a very primitive subterranean temple. In the middle there was a phallus of white stone. Set told me that many incarnations ago I committed a sin against masculine power when I castrated myself. I had done this as an oath of purity and as a sacrifice to Isis, since I was at that time a priest of her temple.

Set left me there and I meditated in front of the white stone until everything dissolved in the white light emanating from it. Once I was able to use my psychic vision again, Set led me through a corridor, and in one niche I saw a dark Isis statue with several arms, like the Hindu Kali. When she came to life, I told her that my present understanding of purity was different, as well as the fact that my understanding of her had also changed. I am now able to see purity in the midst of worldly activities. I know she represents material existence, and now I can worship her within all the sacraments of the world. She let me pass, and I felt Isis would manifest in my physical life in the future. When Set and I returned to the Hall of Justice, I was weighed and found flawless.

Set appeared again as a gigantic erect crocodile. He then led me through corridors where there were slaves working. Then we emerged into a passage which ended in outer space. There he asked me to remember that he was also a cosmic force, the one dealing with matter. I felt I made a great connection with him.

This meditation untangled me from physical blockages with women, but it also caused a shift in my consciousness. From then on I was subconsciously waiting for the Goddess to manifest in my life. I opened the roads in that meditation for the Goddess to express herself fully in the three-dimensional world. Even so, the ascetic side of me didn't believe that She would come as a permanent contact with a real woman. I never let my mind wander in romantic daydreaming, but the manifestation of the

Goddess in my physical life has proven to be beyond anything I could have expected those days.

On November 15, 1988, I coordinated a grand magical ceremony for an evocation of Isis; the aim of my group was to bring her down to earth as much as possible for the welfare of humanity. This was done with five powerful collaborators. I had written down the ceremony based on the structure of the Hexagram. There was a triangle of Male Initiates: Osiris [the Egyptian Sun-God of Eternity, husband of Isis]; Thoth [the Egyptian God of Science, Arts, and Magic, protector of Isis]; and Horus [Her warrior son]. Calling the manifestation of the three aspects of Isis was the White Isis, Her highest, most-cosmic aspect; the Black Isis, Her aspect as builder of forms and regulator of the pure force of the Spirit; and the Multi-colored Isis, or She who bears the powers of Mother Nature.

The White and the Black Isis were incarnated in the ritual by two of my students who were natural psychics and remember past incarnations as priestesses of Isis. The Multi-colored Isis was enacted by my powerful sixty-year-old magical partner, who had devoted all her life to helping human evolution. For the roles of Osiris and Thoth, two men with very strong auras were present. I represented Horus.

We all had agreed that our task in the ceremony would be to materialize as much as possible the presence of Isis in the world, but the exquisite psychic atmosphere that came over us and saturated the temple during the magical work was so overwhelming, that the magicians lost concentration on the purpose of the ceremony. They fell into ecstasy; the bliss eroded their mental focus. Only my magical partner and I held to our will along the whole ceremony with the intention of bringing the Goddess down to earth.

I myself remember resisting the uprising psychic current generated by the bliss of the other people involved. At the end of the ceremony I was exhausted, and when I expressed my dissatisfaction with the turn of the events during the evocation, the participants said they were happy and fulfilled by the spiritual contact as it happened, and didn't expect anything else from it. That was not enough for me; I even got into an argument with one of the priestesses who considered the energies of Isis so pure they could never materialize in the coarseness of matter. In her opinion to bring Isis down to the material plane would mean to desecrate Her pure essence.

I was certain about the need to unite the spiritual and material worlds, but the priestess replied that she as a woman knew better what Isis wanted. I challenged her to settle our dispute by consulting the Goddess through the Tarot and the I Ching. If the answers of both divination systems indicated materialization, that would mean Isis wanted to manifest in the world of matter and I was correct; if the answers were about spiritual fulfillment and retreat, the priestess would win. We spread the cards and threw the Chinese coins. Both divination systems answered as clearly as they possibly could that the Goddess would manifest shortly in the future.

On November 18, 1988, I wrote in my magical diary:

"I have not meditated since the ceremony of Nov. 15, but today I entered my temple and did a short invocation to my 'contacts.' Isis appeared so clearly between the columns of my temple! I could feel her standing in an almost physical body in front of me. My heart was totally open, pouring love by tons toward her. She told me she would come into my life because I was the only one really calling for her in the ceremony; that I am a 'cosmic magician' temporarily operating under physical laws; that I have been with her always and will always be." The feeling that she would become something real for me in the near future was overwhelming.

Some of the visions were giving me cues about how my life would change when I met with my Twin Soul, although I was not quite able to interpret them in this light. The following one, taken from my record of magic was clearly telling me that the eagle was now an ally. The other meaning of the heraldic eagle was the imperial bloodline I was soon going to meet in Luisa, my Twin Soul. Luisa is an Austrian citizen, and the eagle in this vision closely resembled that of the Austrian flag before the modifications introduced under socialism.

On Nov. 19, 1988, I wrote: "While on the bus going to Mexicali and after a spontaneous burst of adoration to Isis, I had a conscious reverie in which I saw Isis and Osiris merging. At the same time I was unconsciously asking 'Who am I?' they became one; an egg opened in a black sky with a magnetic white sun. From the egg a double-headed blue heraldic eagle emerged. On the beak it had a scepter and a triple cross; in its claws it held an orb and a sword."

Three days later I received on the same spot a graphic symbol to channel the double-headed eagle energies to earth. All my magnetic healing patients were able to feel the power of this symbol.

On Nov. 30 I saw Anubis in my meditation, and he told me I would be trained in power from then on. On Jan. 5, 1989, Isis came to me in my psychic vision. She gave me a book entitled *The Cosmic Miracles*, about the stars and constellations and their powers. This was another premonition concerning the work my Twin Soul and I would set ourselves to do upon meeting on the physical plane: *STAR*LIFE Cosmic Activations*, our system for human empowerment.

The magical work in the meditation room of the United Nations building opened me to telepathic contact with three of the Masters of the Transhimalayan Brotherhood. I found out later that two of these Masters had been in communication with Luisa for a long time before we met. Count St. Germain, also known as Prince Rackozi, was one of them.

My first telepathic contact with Count St. Germain occurred in 1986. I was in a conscious dream and asked to know who was the Transhimalayan Master I was working with. I saw a very handsome man on the streets of New York. And I simply knew it was St. Germain. Before awakening I asked him to give me proof that my vision was correct. The next day I went to visit a group that met every week to discuss esoteric philosophy. I had not been with them for nearly a year and it took me by surprise when upon entering I was given a folded piece of paper. They told me they were having a drawing that day and the winner would get the small wrapped gift on the table. I had the winning number; the book was *The Golden Book of St. Germain*.

In 1989 after my return from New York and the United Nations ritual (described in the previous chapter), I felt Count St. Germain suddenly coming into my mental field as I entered my healing office. His wavelength had the purity of diamond light. "I will take you to move and live among nobility. You will be as a part of me. Those will be difficult days, but you should prevail," he said. The contact was very strong, but the message sounded as if it were just a fantasy. I did not know anyone of nobility, and at that time I was not thinking that I would live outside of México. It was only three months later that I found out Luisa was indeed a direct descendant of the Rackozi family, and that she also had received telepathic contacts from her ancestor years before we met.

During the next few days after the magical operation at the United Nations building, I received two Initiations into two different Hermetic groups, these initiations enabling the one who received them to make closer contact with the Invisible Hierarchy in charge of the organization which conferred them. One of these initiations took place in Philadelphia. It was a beautiful ceremony with about thirty people. In the drama of the Judgment of Osiris in the Underworld I played the part of Osiris, who had to answer forty-two questions from the Lords of Karma and at the end is found pure and becomes immortal.

Those days my life was very busy and exciting, but the night after this ceremony I entered into a state of sadness, longing for a companion on the spiritual road. I realized that I had students and some friends, but nobody really shared my perspective of life, nobody understood my ideals. I saw it was nearly impossible to find someone as ardent and as advanced on the path. I realized how difficult it would be to find a compatible woman who was already daring and experienced on the path of High Magic.

I cried, then asked Anubis, the invisible guide of the organization which initiated me that day, "The Opener of the Ways," to open the path of my life to a companion with whom I could share my most intimate thoughts, a soul as similar to mine as possible in a woman's body. I felt it would be granted, but I couldn't imagine how.

Magic works in strange synchronistic ways. My begging for a spiritual companion had happened only a few days after Luisa had been given my address. I cried to the Opener of the Ways on April 20th; Luisa dated her first letter to me April 17th.

When I returned to México her letter was waiting for me. The moment I touched it, without even reading the sender's name, I saw a golden arch of light which started in my heart and was lost beyond the horizon, wherever she was located. At that time I interpreted that vision as a spiritual connection between teacher and student. In that letter she was asking me to supervise her daily Kabalistic meditations. In fact, she was an advanced student of the same organization that initiated me on April 20th!

I formally answered Luisa and asked that she send me her spiritual diaries as soon as possible because I had recently bought tickets for a trip to India and Egypt. I had the feeling my life was about to change; I was ready for something new. The Masters had told me through telepathic contact to cut the links with my present environment and free myself up for travel and "work on a planetary scale."

In my second letter to Luisa I wrote: "This is strange. I feel a strong spiritual connection with you, but I do not know you yet." It puzzled me how I had developed an intense affection just by reading about her Kabalistic meditations. However, I was concerned with my trip and did not have time for any other idea to cross my mind.

My energy field was changing dramatically, too. The angels of love were revealing themselves to me. The following are sections of my magical diary:

June 5. I was doing biomagnetic healing work and after 45 minutes of treating a patient, I entered into a high state of consciousness. I felt a presence in the room and let myself drift into communication with it.

The presence had the shape of "The Hermit" in the Tarot cards, but the energy was that of an angel, not an Initiate. He told me he was giving me the gift of happiness, that I could be forever happy from now on. Everything was white light; the being transformed himself into an emerald of magnificent color. At the end he told me my new name was "Benithish."

Later, using numerological Kabala I found the number of "Benithish" to be 777, the triple force of the sephira, or emanation of divine force, associated with Venus, this planet also associated with happiness and the emerald.

June 7. I checked the ephemeris. On June 5, the day of my new name, Venus was indeed transiting over zero degree of Cancer, just a degree-and-a-half away from the cusp of my First House. . .so every factor leads to the conclusion the contact was genuine.

June 8. Today Venus is transiting my Part of Fortune, so I decided to invoke the Goddess to bring love into my life, and I did an Enochian invocation to the powers of the 7th æther.

First, I received the pure energy of Aphrodite; next, the same Hermit angel of June 5 appeared to me. This time he told me that my life was changing, my strongly based Hermit energy was leaving me. I won't be a hermit anymore. The new archetype acting upon my personality is "La Force" of the Tarot cards.

And then. . .the woman from the Eleventh Major Arcana of the Tarot came in... Wow! It was not the pure, white-dressed lady of the traditional card; she was the sexiest, most fiery goddess I have ever found. She was Shakti [the Hindu goddess of manifested existence], she was Babalon [the goddess of substance and desire in Crowley's cosmology]. She also changed into a fiery-red sensuous Dakini [Tibetan goddess of happiness and passion] who entered my body and made me move like a flame. She was everywhere.

She blasted me with energy. I was astonished, enjoying, but sometimes concerned about how to keep all this power under control. The recurrent idea was that I will stop being a hermit and live in her energy-field over the next years. This new archetype is giving me the vision of the Naked Venus, just as the one Christian Rosencreutz had. I will be able to unify Illuminism and Hedonism in my life, and that sounds like fun!

June 12. . . .and then a feminine voice, from the goddess contacted on June 8th, spoke softly to me: "Be the supreme commander. You are in charge, and I'm the Voice of Wisdom to guide you. I'm always with you from now on."

I was so immersed in my psychic world I was not yet aware who the link was for all these contacts. I was blind to the fact that Luisa was the physical manifestation of the Goddess coming to my universe. It was wonderful that Luisa and I had both kept records of our inner experiences and the letters we sent to each other during that period.

The same June 12th, Luisa wrote to me: "I also feel a strong connection with you...It scares and confuses me...I think of you all the time! Also I felt your presence around me many times these

THE HEART OF THE SERPENT

three days...All this confuses me a lot. I do not even know you yet!"

On June 13th she wrote: "I feel closer and closer to you every day! It is an obliterating sensation!...If you know, if you feel the same...please explain this to me!"

I answered her on June 16th: "So you are also feeling the Unconditional Love that everybody theorizes about, eh?...You ask for an explanation of this. I do not know if this is necessary, but I will try:

I could explain all this with the much-abused subject of the previous incarnations in which we knew each other. That could be, but there is a more thorough explanation: You and I already know each other on our higher levels, beyond Time and Space.

Since we have a similar vibration on the higher levels we are now connecting little by little on the denser levels, as if our spirit is One and the same at the top of a gigantic zipper, and this zipper is gently closing, joining its two halves, or what we are on the physical level."

Surely I wrote this moved by higher inspiration. From the level of my five senses I would never dare to say this to a woman if I didn't even know how she looked! Let alone the fact that in my rational mind I was already heading toward the Himalayas and the Egyptian temples.

On June 25th Luisa wrote the following lines in her magical records: "The Starlords said, on top of all that I wrote for the meditation: 'Luis is Amoun, as you have always known him. You can trust him! Believe us, he is him. And we have a small present for you: We will give him the exact information that we are giving you, and sooner than you think, you will be comparing results with one another! He is your Twin Soul for whom you so long!'"

This information came to her from beings who are the manifestation, on a human psychic level, of the souls of the stars. She had been in close relationship with another astral being, an Egyptian priest called Amoun, who appeared often in dreams, meditations, and even in her daily life for the past eight years. She had never seen a picture of me, but after this revelation, she understood that this higher, magical part of me had been with her for a long time.

Later, when we met and compared our written materials, I could clearly see how it was the same for me, the manifestations of the Goddess in my life were projections of Luisa's divine essence. I know all women have a higher divine essence, an archetypal Goddess power behind their human personality; but I'm certain very few women are so transparent to the Goddess that their divine essence can be as powerful and close to the physical plane as Luisa's.

The following two extracts from our magical diaries before we met illustrate how close our telepathic communion was on the higher levels:

On July 3rd I wrote in my magical records: "On June 30th I did an Invocation to Osiris. On July 1st I meditated for a long time on the Egyptian planes of consciousness. Isis came, and at one point I was seeing with her, both of us of monumental size, out of Time and Space, the 'Mirror of Creation,' the illusion of the manifested universe. We saw it as something flat as compared to the richness of Eternity.

Then I, from my higher self, contracted all that sense of freedom and power into my physical atoms, and decided to have those qualities in my life."

On July 13th Luisa wrote: "We concentrated in the here and now and he [Luis] told me to go higher and higher. We left the solar system behind and came to the center of the galaxy and the center of the cosmos.

Here the feeling of 'I am' is even greater. It feels as if this Eternal Now expands us and compresses us at the same time!"

We were sharing the same levels of consciousness, but they were coming down to the rational mind through slightly different symbols. Luisa understood the miracle of our spiritual relationship sooner than I did. At this time I was still unable to find the connection between the Goddess and Luisa. I had several reasons for blocking my mind whenever the thought of a romance with Luisa crept into my rational mind:

֍ She was my student.

֍ She was married.

֍ I didn't know how she looked.

֍ I didn't really want to fall in love yet since the scars of my previous marriage were still fresh.

I was aware of the fantasy that many New Agers engage in regarding Twin Souls, Soulmates, Twin Flames, etc. I always thought the idea of soulmates was a stupid naive excuse to postpone happiness and to avoid the responsibility of being independent. Self-reliance was my word in these matters.

So when on July 17th she wrote: "I feel all my being vibrating with a single vibration: my love for you!"—I got really concerned. I was amazed how a woman could trust her instincts to such an extent. She hadn't even seen me in a photograph! All she had were three or four letters from me. I even thought a woman with such drive and power might be dangerous!

I wrote back with five good reasons for her to consider the possibility that she was deluding herself. The letter had a diplomatic tone of discouragement, but my intuition flashed in it for a few seconds when I wrote: "I had the idea that in the future you and I might write a book on Stellar and Polarity Magic." She replied to me that she would keep her emotions under control, but she felt strongly that we had a mission to accomplish since the cosmic levels of consciousness she reached when we were united in the higher realms had never been described before in any book; it was her duty to inform others about them.

The following passages in my magical diary demonstrate the psychic transformation I underwent before meeting Luisa on the physical plane:

July 16. I saw Agni [The God of Fire in Hindu-Tibetan mythology] burning my castle [the place I always visualized when meditating]. Then he told me I had been appointed to another place. I was raised vertically to a circle of white-dressed people above the clouds.

July 21. Another angel, "The Angel of Eternal Love," gives me a powerful symbol for bringing down his energy into the atmosphere around me. This angel asked me if I wanted to be his representative on earth. . .That's fine with me!

July 25. Last night, just before falling asleep, I received the message that I should dismantle my magical temple. The Goddess appears and fills my consciousness. She says I should begin a new era of magic, without too much intellect, but the pure radiation of my love to Her. . .That my work is not anymore the cross in the circle, but the point of expansive flame in the circle of Her love, no directions, only pure being. That I might call the spirits of Joy to fill the space between the point and the circle.

July 26. Wham!!! I was overshadowed by the Goddess. I was Her, feeling the spark of my dear child, Luis, traveling through my monumental body; this gave me divine pleasure. And afterwards an overwhelming universal feeling of love and warmth and protection. I felt for a few moments I was Her, thinking about my personal self, about "my baby Luis." I will never forsake him, no matter how old he gets I will be always around him. I will always spoil him!. . .

When the transference of consciousness faded, I received instructions for a new ritual: I should wear a red robe and keep a sword in my hand. In this ritual I am Flame, Fire, Light, Radiance in the center; She is the blue circle all around me. I should fill the space between the point (me) and the circle (Her) with aromatic herbs, representing the spirits of Joy, our sons. I then call the Solar force in me. I become all Light and the Fire of Love, and use the spiral pattern to get to the limits of the circle and bring Her to the point, making Beingness and Not-beingness become ONE.

Last thing She told me was that She will be my magical tutor from now on, that Anubis has handed me to Her as one of his graduate students. I know the key to her magic is fluidity. I'm thrilled with the new adventure!. . .

Two hours later: I pondered about the symbolism of this ceremony; it seems to be a perfect representation of the powers behind the previous June 8th contact with "The Force" Tarot symbol. In that card the Woman of the Infinite is expanding (opening) the power (jaws) of the solar symbol (lion).

On August 5th, the morning of my trip to Denver when I met Luisa, upon awakening I heard the beautiful voice of the Goddess, "Today is the first day of your new life. I have a surprise for you!"

I never let my thoughts wander before about my relationship with Luisa, but flying to Denver was an ordeal of concentration. I was traveling with a student and friend of mine. We were to attend a seminar about advanced magic. It was very difficult to keep talking to my friend since my mind was obsessed with the idea of meeting Luisa. I knew Luisa would be there. I could hardly wait!

I was such a jerk. I decided to test her. If she was such a good psychic, I wanted to know how long she would need to figure out where I was in a room full of other attendants of the seminar. She didn't know how I looked. . . Would she recognize my energy in such a distracting environment? Or would she try to find someone who looked Mexican, which is not evident in my case. I couldn't control myself long enough to put the stupid test into action. The moment I saw her I jumped from my seat as if struck by lightning! Her energy was so vibrant and intense it was out of this world. Our auras became one sealed unit when I introduced myself to her. Instant recognition, instant familiarity. From that day on we got many more contacts with the invisible guides and new energies at our disposal—then we knew we had a mission. We would be together; all the doors would be open; all the information would be given. We were recognized as part of those from the subtle levels who opened the ways for us to meet.

☙☙☙☙☙☙☙☙☙☙☙

7

THE DISCOVERY OF MY MISSION

Life accelerates in our times, and this fact itself is physical evidence of the gigantic vibrational change our planet is undergoing at the end of this millennium.

The New Age community firmly believes the earth is being contacted by beings from many places and dimensions. These beings all agree that something big is about to happen. Some groups call it the acceptance of our planetary consciousness within the "Galactic Federation"; others say earth is suffering an initiation that will transform it into a sacred planet in the near future. Everybody in the metaphysical community envisions this to occur in synchrony with a change in human consciousness. It is expected that average humanity will cast away its obsolete thought processes, breaking the shells of egocentrism, ethnocentrism, and materialism.

How will this miracle happen? The living planet on which we live is raising and enforcing the new human perspective through diverse corrective measures. It filters its influence through global economics, politics, and ecology. The soul of our planet is forcing humanity to make survival choices requiring expanded collective awareness and forethought.

Instruction for change also comes in a positive way through the many who are now awakening. Those who are closer to the source by virtue of complex karmic laws have a message to share, a social mission of an evolutionary nature.

The Enochian angels told me during the magical retreat in 1987 that I would receive a system to bring the ancient esoteric teachings into contemporary style. In countless other visions I was given the mission of bringing the Cosmic Fire from the stars to our planet.

It wasn't until I met Luisa that I actually initiated my mission. She inspired me; she reinforced the trust I had in myself; she acted as a mirror for the best in me. She helped me to launch the STAR*LIFE project with all that she had.

I had been given my part to play in the evolutionary drama. Parts of this information came in telepathic communication with the invisible guides of humanity, sometimes, however, I got the seeds of wisdom from that place of Unity where every question has its answer. When this happened, these seeds of truth unfolded their paradoxical beingness, and I learned that the truths received were only a temporary point of convergence, a relative position within vast moving forces that higher consciousness perceives as synthetic and all inclusive.

I am well aware that the evolutionary drama is just one way to give meaning and a sense of direction to life; from other levels of awareness, there is no drama to play. Whatever happens in the world is irrelevant to the dimensions of eternal stability I have accessed at times. So I have played a part in earth's evolutionary drama because it helps me to define my human self, because it allows me to connect with life in a constructive way, and because I enjoy it.

My sense of mission is just an ephemeral convergence of social and personal meanings. It was fruitful for me and is valuable for those who are benefiting from STAR*LIFE; it still gives me a sense of identity and helps me to learn more about sacrifice, sharing, and interdependence. Nevertheless, in the vastness of the transpersonal regions I am now able to access, I have learned not to get caught in the role my mission requires me to play. Now I can both maintain several interpretations of life and understand my function on each level... simultaneously. Yet this does not suggest lack of integrity; it is simply that I have developed a deeper perception.

From one of these levels of interpretation, the one validated as I actualized my mission, I am, as many other spiritual warriors, a spark from another solar system who chose to help in the catalysis of the planet's evolution in times of great change. I can see myself as a knight in shining armor against the dark forces of stagnation and decay. This is not a delusion; the changes in my students is my best advertisement.

I also know myself as the incarnation of an archetypal force with a cosmic function: that of bringer of enlightenment and growth. Although this is not evident at all times, it is simply a natural expression of my true nature.

From another viewpoint, I am a product of our times—part of a dissatisfied generation looking for every possible alternative to transcend the human condition, sometimes with positive results.

From another, more-inclusive level of interpretation, I am nothing. I have also seen my temporal manifestation as a shell, a puppet, a by-product of the interplay of inconceivable forces set into activity since the beginning of time with predetermined results my mind can only guess.

From the highest perspective, I simply am. I am learning not to define myself too seriously because every definition is a limitation. I want to remain open to growth, and besides, I also realized long ago the infinitude of my being.

All this said, I will try to describe my contribution to humankind and the worries, joys, and surprises in its making.

In my visions I have seen a cosmic wave of fiery energy and the earth moving through it. This cosmic wave causes planetary acceleration of all its processes; it emphasizes the good and the bad as well. This cosmic process corresponds to a Biblical sentence stating that at the end of time (i.e., for the Christian era) those who have will get more, and those who don't will have taken away what little they do have. Our civilization is not only producing more geniuses and visionaries, but also more tyrants and mental patients. Big cities, which correspond to energetic focal points within the earth, are spectacular displays of both human posibilities: the worst and the best. This is the time when, if you are going up, you will go up more quickly; if you are going down, you will fall faster. This is the time of decisions.

The positive side of this planetary process creates a time of power. For good or bad, power is here, and we have to learn to live with it. Gone are the days when all that you needed to feel at ease was to be morally praiseworthy, socially appreciated, and conventionally good enough to gain heaven after your death.

The responsibilities of today's human beings are complex. You, as everyone else, are now aware of pressure coming from your inner urges, your personal motivations, your original (meaning "from the origin") drives. You might not know what these are yet, but you have a deep dissatisfaction with your life as it is; you yearn for something else, and as long as you don't know what the Real You wants, contemporary advertising will keep manipulating your inner need for change into socially acceptable and—for the advertisers—economically profitable achievements.

Inner pressure is pure power, power to actualize your Real Self. However, most people do not know what to look for. They are misinformed about the potential of human life. They are repressed by the social standards of past generations, so the power for self-actualization manifests in convoluted ways, producing distinct personality characteristics, but not creating a full effect, an original direction. Most people set themselves to analyze, evaluate, judge, and criticize their differences, trapping their young, emerging natural powers into rigid mental structures.

I came to this planet because this is a time of power. I came with the mission of teaching others how to handle this power. That's why I am primarily an instructor of magic. For me magic is an art, the art of handling power. As a painter uses colors and a musician sounds, a magus uses energies, powers. Every artist intends to create a masterpiece. The masterpiece of the magus is his/her own life.

Magic is for me the way to actualize, to express, to set into motion the will of the Higher Self. Some use magical procedures to actualize egotistical drives of the personality, but it always happens that the weak and transitory footing of their efforts crumbles down in the end. When all the constructions of the "me" break down, they learn about the continuous source of power that is available once they align with their real selves.

Magic for me is neither opposed to religion nor to logic and contemporary scientific opinions, as long as they don't oppose the will of the Higher Self. Sometimes they do, and then I always stand on the side of magic.

Magic is not necessarily ritual or ceremony. It is the focus of all that you are in the single direction of inner divine will. This can be accomplished in many ways.

STAR*LIFE is the system I created to take people along the path of magic in a stable, balanced way. I envision the STAR*LIFE project as the embodiment of a majestic being comprised of the consciousness of the spiritual beings I have contacted in the past, those who gave me their codes to access their essence at will. They, as a single collective mind, manifest into three-dimensional reality through the human frequencies of the activated STAR*LIFE practitioners.

In a sense, the earthly body of STAR*LIFE is that of the hundreds of activated students. What they are and what they express is now intermingled with the essence of the angels to whom they are attuned. The synergy of this collective mystical union should create a resonance in the collective consciousness of humanity, and through it to the other kingdoms of nature. In this way, the whole planet is indirectly subjected to cosmic frequencies through the cosmic activation of a few of His creatures.

I see myself as the temporary point of convergence between angelic and human consciousness, activating and educating those on earth, building bridges for manifestation for those beyond. I stand at the exact point where the pyramid of humanity and the inverted cone of the spirit meet—as a mediator between worlds.

STAR*LIFE is a path of human development with an emphasis on power. Love, wisdom, and power are the individual petals on the full bloom of balanced spiritual growth. They are associated with complete development of the emotional, mental, and physical dimensions of human beings. However, most people associate spirituality only with love and wisdom; this is based on the old falsehood that achievement on the physical plane is opposed to salvation or liberation from the material world. Power is regarded as something dangerous for the spiritual path, and it is. Nevertheless, it is an essential ingredient in the harmonious growth of consciousness.

There are many paths to enlightenment which emphasize love. The mystical approach is always the safest, although I have seen countless examples of imbalance on this path as well as on others. Those of a mystical nature are easily caught in the polarity of that which belongs to the divine world—their meditation time, their church or temple, their guru, saving the dolphins or unspoiled areas of nature—as opposed to that which is profane, impure, or material, such as their jobs and other ties with the everyday world. I have counseled hundreds of students of devotional systems who have a very difficult time integrating their spiritual views into their Western lifestyle. They lack the power to bring their visions into objective existence.

The spiritual paths which emphasize wisdom are those that focus on a given cosmology or belief system and aim at the development of the abstract levels of the mind by meditating on truths of a cosmic order or by silencing the discursive mind. Generally speaking, Kabalah, theosophy, and many Buddhist sects are in this category. The danger for those who think wisdom is the only road to Nirvana is bondage to the interpretive faculties of the mind. Many get caught in the letter, in the method, in the classification, in the dogma. There is a spiritual pride that comes from knowing the many levels and cosmic laws of the universe. It is easy to mistake the knowing about with the experience itself. Even if some have had revelations of the kingdom of heaven in the past, thinking about what happened then will not bring these experiences back to life.

The paths which emphasize power have always been condemned in the past, and today are still suspect. I can understand; those suspicions are partially correct.

Human society is based on predictability, order, and rhythm. Unfortunately, humanity's definition of order is very limited. Great changes are always products of higher rhythms; but, until they are established, they are regarded as chaos and feared. If you are on a path which emphasizes power, you align (consciously or unconsciously) with these higher rhythms wherein the power lies. When power comes to you in the beginning, so does chaos. Your life, therefore, loses predictability for a time; it is this frequency of unpredictability in your aura which others feel and fear intuitively. Those who are oriented toward stability might experience severe unconscious reactions when in your presence. They will always find good reasons to avoid and/or criticize you, but the truth is that they are reacting against you out of their own fears.

The power coming to you which causes ripples in your auric field not only disturbs your old thoughtforms, but also those of others around you. So for awhile you are in conflict, inside and outside. This is the first ordeal of power.

Later, when the cosmic fire you invoked has purified enough of your energy matrix, it will flow out with force, focus, and continuity. When you sound your own note loud and clear, everything around you will resonate with it. You will be creating your personal universe in this way.

Here you will be walking the razor's edge of power. On one side lies the abyss of spiritual arrogance that your sense of achievement will invariably bring. On the other waits the abyss of the feelings of ineffectuality that come with the realization that any achievement is only a temporary landmark on a never-ending road.

There are higher plateaus on the paths of love, wisdom, and power; there are also stages where this distinction becomes irrelevant since everything merges into a harmonious fluidity between the objective and subjective levels of perception. Even so, it is necessary in the early stages to keep an eye on a balanced development of these three aspects of spiritual life.

In STAR*LIFE students do not have to train to have access to the energies from the invisible levels. The spiritual beings I established communication with gave me the power to manifest and anchor their frequencies in the energy matrix of my students so that they themselves can call forth the energies whenever they draw in the air a symbol with their hands.

The transference of the ability to draw the energies is accomplished through a process I call "Cosmic Activation." During a

Cosmic Activation I expand my awareness to include all there is. From this exalted non-localized state, free of the perception of time, space, substance, form, etc., I call the cosmic force I want to activate in my student by the use of the codes given to me at the time of the first contact. As the invoked force makes itself felt everywhere in my field of awareness, I align with my original cosmic function: I become a catalyzer! My universal will then focuses on the higher spiritual layers of the auric field of my student and a merging that I can't quite describe takes place. In it the invoked cosmic force and the abstract levels of my student become one. More I cannot explain. The Cosmic Activations were given in the beginning only in private one-hour sessions. Later I discovered I was able to confer them telepathically with exactly the same results. Now they are also given in group consecration ceremonials as a way to introduce people to the classic arts of magic.

During my magical retreat of 1987 the Enochian angels predicted I would organize my teachings around the five metaphysical elements and two other avenues for the expansion of awareness that have not been disclosed to the public yet. They were correct; two years later I structured STAR*LIFE on three levels. The first one deals with the five elemental energies of the universe.

The metaphysical elements are the modalities of energy that condition material existence. They can properly be called the spectrum of energies of the Holy Spirit, or the Goddess, or of Universal Substance.

Sages of all cultures have known about these five fundamental energies for millennia: the Hindu called them the Tattwas, the Tibetans named them the Dignities, the Chinese study them as the Five Phases of energy, and in the Western esoteric tradition, they are the same as the four metaphysical elements and the Æther: the cross with Jesuschrist or the rose in its center, Tetragrammaton, or the lost name of God. In the Native

American Indian tradition they are the four winds and the place of rest in the center of the Medicine Wheel.

The metaphysical elements bridge the spiritual and material worlds for the Magus. It is through the power of the metaphysical elements that the Magus brings changes to his world according to the visions he receives from the higher dimensions.

Shamans and Hermetic, Tibetan, Ayurvedic (East Indian), and Chinese doctors have also used the knowledge of the five metaphysical elements in diagnosing and healing their patients. When the metaphysical elements are in balance, health is reestablished.

The conceptual foundation of the energy work with the elemental energies of the first level is still cause and effect oriented. Practitioners bring one or several elemental energies to balance or clear away distorted energies, as well as to purify the chakras and etheric channels. On the other hand, the second level of STAR*LIFE is as different from the first as quantum physics is from Newtonian physics.

Working with the archetypal energies of the second level introduces students to a vastly different perspective. It changes the interpretation of personal reality in ways that expand appreciation of life and an understanding of their individual function on this planet.

The effect of the archetypal forces invoked by the procedures of the second level of STAR*LIFE is very powerful. It is absolutely dynamic, highly meaningful work. Here students learn to communicate with the archetypal beings using the symbols of ancient Greek theurgy, and avail themselves of these energies to transform their lives.

I believe that the use of the archetypal energies of the second level of STAR*LIFE is a very effective way to balance the influence of negative astrological configurations in natal horoscopes, progressions, or transits. The Cosmic Activations and attendant procedures act as polarizing filters for the aura so that the disturbing energies of negative planetary aspects will manifest only in a subdued form.

This is not to say that once students take the Cosmic Activations they are automatically safe from crisis. Change will continue, even faster than before as the new energy level accelerates growth on many levels. Some of this change might still be painful for the personality, but the knowledge that they have the tool to work with the emerging issues makes a big difference in the interpretation of the event. They are no longer victims of karma, but fully equipped warriors who thrill at the challenge that life presents.

The third level of STAR*LIFE deals with the energies of the stars and constellations. These energies have a level of refinement that can only be perceived by extraordinary sensitives or after enough experience with the elemental and archetypal energies. All of the third-level energies have royal qualities. They transmit feelings of supremacy and immutability, as if you were allowed to experience supreme perfection.

It is very difficult to find words to describe the stellar energies. For example, the Cosmic Activation of Aldebaran evokes the feeling of raw power and absolute will very much as the Kings of Mesopotamia probably experienced. The Cosmic Activation of Regulus brings a warm, noble feeling, perhaps similar to the energy surrounding Richard the Lion-Hearted or Charlemagne. The Cosmic Activation of Deneb, a star in the Swan Constellation, brings a feeling of aesthetic ecstasy, or supreme sophistication comparable to the ambience surrounding Louis XIV.

According to esoteric philosophy, the feelings condition the perceptions and are the real cause of karma. So holding one's attention on any of the exalted feelings associated with the application of the stellar energies manifests those qualities in everyday life. Life will reflect the qualities of energy you project. This is a metaphysical truth.

There is also a feeling of infinitude that permeates all the energies of the third level. This helps to mantain the student's consciousness on its true level, that is, the unlimited.

When I started the whole STAR*LIFE system I underwent all the levels of worry, anxiety, and disbelief associated with any new project. It wasn't easy to go out to the New Age marketplace and advertise my outlandish skills. It wasn't easy to define a price for my services. For months, while I was writing the literature that comes with every degree, I felt the invectives of the cosmic fire. It was a strange fiery sensation on the subtle levels of my aura, beyond the mental and emotional layers, an abstract flame burning mercilessly innumerable facets of defeat and victimization over many lifetimes. My physical body writhed, and I felt agonizing abstract pain all around me, that would come to nothing as suddenly as it had started.

Luisa was having her own ordeal at the same time. Her blue-blooded family was using all the emotional pressure at their disposal to force her to change her mind about our upcoming union. They disapproved of our marriage, which, nevertheless, was accomplished first on the Isle of Jersey, and then in America the next year. Luisa's challenge was several times more difficult than mine: she left behind the castles and the European jet-set to join her destiny to a Mexican with an uncertain future. She endured scorn and isolation as a warrior and a martyr, fighting for her inner truth, with her eyes fixed on our dreams.

Now my work as a cosmic activator is full of wonders. It has allowed me to relate to highly evolved individuals. People who after years of training in systems emphasizing love or wisdom were ready for the actual experience of the things they could only read about in books.

In many cases I have felt positive karmic links with my students; I have seen the Serpent of Life biting its own tail. The Cosmic Activations of today are superimposed on the timeless dimensions over initiations into the same frequencies undergone in sacred places or temples from my students' previous lives.

I am, in my function as a Cosmic Activator, an eternal point of convergence between the higher and the lower—a wonderful perspective that is difficult to describe. I have found my position in the universal scheme. That is my mission for this lifetime.

When I recede into the highest planes I know I am everything, but in the operative dimensions of the universe my function is to be an intermediary, a conscious and willing agent of the cosmic rhythms, and a conductor of souls into the eternal.

Now I can see how my True Self directed my human life the way it did, how having the life I had was essential for modeling a proper psychological vehicle capable of the spiritual function entrusted to me from the beginning.

☙☙☙☙☙☙

8

BUSINESS AS USUAL

My work in applied metaphysics allows me to travel and meet interesting people. This chapter is about some of the most unique energy-consciousness configurations that I have seen in my students and clients. I'm not a clairvoyant all the time. Thank God! I open my Third Eye at will and get information only about what I focus on.

In diagnosing my students' energy fields, the first thing I observe is the area above the head. I see something there that resembles inverted cones made of colored light; the wider area of the cones extends into infinity and disappears from my sight about two to three yards above the head; the apex of the cones usually penetrates into the head. There are variations on this, some of which will be dealt with later.

Most people have two or three different-colored cones. Although the cones are layered inside each other, they are translucent, allowing me to see the inner ones. The cones change very little during the span of a life. They represent the basic incoming qualities of energy with which an individual is born.

Based on the cones' position, color, width, and brilliance, I receive information about the basic personality traits and areas of action where each can develop his/her full potential. I always counsel people based on these intrinsic predispositions and warn that they should not be acted against. For example, if someone has a prominent yellow cone, indicating a cold, analytical mind and an introverted and predictable personality, no matter how diligently this person might try to be an artist, success in this field will be out of his/her reach.

I first read about these cones in *Human Energy Systems* by Jack Schwarz. Years later I had a private interview with this remarkable man, and somehow in the course of the meeting my Third Eye resonated with his extraordinary frequency. After a few days I developed the ability to see the cones. Without a conscious effort, he empowered me with one of his many talents.

I have seen the cones in twelve basic colors—ten of them align with what is known in esoteric literature as the seven rays. The first and second rays are a combination of two and three colors respectively; rays three to seven have one color each. The colors I see outside the range of the seven rays are indigo and black. Indigo appears in the crown chakras of those who have a cosmic, extraterrestrial heritage, but I will come back to this color later. Black, however, is more than a ray; it is an area in the energy field that resembles a void, although in some cases it takes on a satiny quality of its own. When I see this in people I know they are going through a big transition that can take years to complete. At this time they are aligned with the destroyer aspect of God; they are in the process of a death-and-rebirth experience and, for the time being, they cannot find their place anywhere. Their spiritual life might be rich, but their efforts to stabilize a regular human life will fail until another cone with a definitive color comes to replace the black area. Then their lives will follow a new course.

Sometimes I see the cones without a point; the color fades out before it touches the crown chakra. Then I know the particular energy of that cone is recessive. This disposition points at potentials the individual is unaware of for the time being.

The external cones give me information about the personality, i.e., the first impression this person makes on others. The inner cones refer to the private life, as well as to the imprint of the soul.

The pure energies of the cones come down through the aura and manifest through the chakras, which are centers of radiation along the central part of the body. The chakras are usually prevented from expressing the full power of the rays by obstructive thoughtforms.

Thoughtforms are force fields of diverse qualities that produce in the human mind a pull toward a specific set of thoughts, feelings, and consequent behaviors. When they are strong enough they can even create circumstances in life in accordance with their basic frequencies. From the interpretation of these thoughtforms I know the basic ideas that color the perceptions of my student, that is, ideas about themselves, people, and life in general.

There are what we might call positive thoughtforms; they move us to act on our present goals. They manifest as automatic reactions that are helpful to coordinate our lives in the direction we want. Their usefulness, however, is a relative one. Since the goal of spiritual evolution is to be completely open to new circumstances and all thoughtforms set us into patterns, this can mean stagnation into routines. From a higher perspective, thoughtforms are undesirable condensations of the free, unbounded energy of the spirit.

In my energy-diagnosing sessions I concentrate on the old thoughtforms that hinder worldly achievements as well as higher spiritual awareness. I perceive thoughtforms in a variety of ways, but I favor the shamanistic conceptual frame. When I am in this mode I see the thoughtforms as psychic parasites born from negative emotions.

I see the thoughtforms that produce patterns of anger, depression, hopelessness, etc. as semi-independent energy fields lingering in the aura; some of them are like fogs around the chakras. The powerful ones resemble giant amoebas, or ugly creatures of every shape, that project sticky tentacles into the chakras when it is time for them to feed. Others are like hardened balls of dark material that slow the function of the chakras and paralyze action.

Thoughtforms feed on the same emotional frequencies that generated them and induce distortions in perception to achieve the production of those emotions again and again. They milk these emotions from their prey by entangling their own etheric bodies, or their protrusions, into their victim's etheric field. In this way they set into action specific interpretations of circumstances that arouse the concomitant emotions.

Thoughtforms can attach to weak energy fields, can be inherited, or can be transferred by close proximity, including sexual contact. They can also be projected willfully by sorcery techniques.

Over my years of energy healing and counseling experience I have noticed in 85 per cent of my clients a particular thoughtform that It resembles a black jellyfish between the legs. By unraveling the information of this thoughtform I find that it always seems to have appeared at the time of toilet-training when children are forced to learn to control the sphincter in fear of punishment or reprimand.

This is the first lesson in restriction: Children learn to act as grown-ups demand. Yet beyond the cleanliness and order parents want their children to learn, there are other messages implicated in this training, such as, "There is a part of your body we don't like. It is disgusting. You'd better hide it...We are the ones with the power...This is our territory...You do as we say or you are in trouble." These are some of the messages retained in this thoughtform.

The subtle tension of the sphincters produces a permanent tightness in the energy of the same area. This force field of tightness contains all the information relevant to restriction, and will surface in everyday behavior as a tightness of character socially associated with responsibility, maturity, and growth.

As children grow, most restrictive indoctrinations are stored in the same area. When children run, explore their physical limitations in dangerous games, or leave the house without parental consent they often hear: "Stop it!. . . Don't be stupid!... Watch out or you are going to have an accident." The fears of the parents, impressed on the young mind, feed the thoughtform between the legs, making the child cautious, but also making him/her associate displays of self-confidence with negative reactions from the environment. This creates a partial paralysis in the natural flow of energy through the legs and impairs boldness and courage.

Tensions associated with control of sexual behavior are stored in the same area. It is nearly impossible for a teenager to sublimate sexual impulses—the harnessing of sexuality at this age means most of the time avoiding sexual activity out of fear of moral criticism. By this time there is a psychological equation deeply imbedded in the mind: good, clean, worthy = doing what grown-ups say; bad, ugly, shameful = recognizing or following up on natural impulses.

By the time these people have reached maturity, the energy pattern between the legs has settled to such an extent that we can consider them tight-asses. This is no joke; popular wisdom is correct. What popular wisdom might not yet know is that large segments of the world's population suffer from this tight-ass energy syndrome.

Self-righteousness is a mask for fear of disapproval. It is an unconscious shield to hide the shame of the foul smell (both in a psychological as well as a physiological sense) that comes from the dark spot between the legs. And it is not only the disease of isolated individuals, it is also the malady of whole cultures. The thoughtform between the legs manifests as routine behavior, lack of will, lack of creativity, ungrounding, and lack of energy in general that eventually exposes the body to physical disease.

The energy blockage between the legs will hinder any impulse to move ahead. The negative emotions appearing at the time of toilet training are now large enough to produce a view of life as a repressive experience. The feeling is that the job, the spouse, the family life, the government, and everything else has an overpowering, asphyxiating effect—and there is no place to go.

The thoughtform between the legs prevents energy from circulating between the base chakra and the higher chakras along the energy channel at the body's center. The natural flow of energy that keeps the higher chakras of creativity, insight, and will power functioning is impaired, and these functions are diminished or repressed.

The thoughtform between the legs has yet another negative effect. The obstruction weakens the energy flow between the base chakra and the earth; the sense of interconnectedness with the world is severed. Often there is an extrapolation of the old parental relationship to the present relationship with life, and the person has the subconscious belief that the earth (Mother Nature) will not support any movement along unconventional lines. Or even worse, that the possibility of earning a living (since money is crystallized energy coming from Mother Earth) is always threatened by factors beyond your control, such as the country's economic climate or the boss' capricious decisions.

THE HEART OF THE SERPENT

The rigidity of the energy field can also create a direct effect on the physical body. A weak aura is exposed to distorted energies of every kind, which, in turn, can produce physical disease. These diseases give the sufferer further excuses to attach rigidly to the same old lines of thought and behavior until the end of life.

Lack of grounding caused by the thoughtform makes people engage in all sorts of fantasies about alternative ways of life that might happen if, and only if... The truth is that by this time the force field is too sclerotic to manifest these ideals in the physical reality. Sadly, all these painful conditions will be masked in thoughts of righteousness: sacrifice for the family, society, loyalty to the country, etc. These people feel they are good citizens, indeed they are grayish, narrow-minded, good citizens. Maybe they will go to heaven after all since throughout their lives they have been good children of the family, society, the State, and of God the Father as described in the Old Testament.

The truth is that fear is behind their brittle mental structures, preventing them from expressing their original selves. Fear of the unknown creates an unfulfilled life, but this fear is either unrecognized or validated by an overwhelming set of logical and moral reasons.

This is only one example of how a thoughtform may be transmitted down through several generations. There are innumerable modalities of thoughtforms that can be attached to different chakras. There are those I perceive as metal sheets over the heart, screening out its radiance and creating feelings of isolation and egotism. Others affix to the head, making people create a busy, uncoordinated life with lots of things to do that consume all their time and energy, but lead nowhere.

Clients always agree with my descriptions of their interpretations of life, except when their thoughtforms are located above the head. In this case they cannot recognize them; they sincerely think that's the way life is. These dangerous thoughtforms intercept the cosmic energy coming through the crown chakra

LUIS DE LA LAMA

[handwritten margin note: all kinds of fundamentalists Christian, Muslim, etc]

and distort perception at its source. There I sometimes see what I call macro-thoughtforms that constitute a class of their own.

Macro-thoughtforms condition the perceptions, and, therefore, even the realities, of large sections of the world's population; these forms are born from and feed upon the thoughts and emotions of many generations of human beings. Representation of the seven capital sins as devils by the Christian church is a simplistic but effective way to illustrate the semi-automatic consciousness and the self-preserving reflexes of those artificial creatures. One story can illustrate such a case.

One of my students, Mrs. H., is a married woman who is deeply involved in metaphysical work. The first time she saw Mr. Y., she felt what she described as an arrow of energy coming from Y's sexual chakra directly to hers, and after this a continuous intense sensation coming close to an orgasm. The man had barely talked to her, but her sensations were so strong that she set out to find out more about it.

H. and Y. met about six times as friends. As the man was making strong advances toward her, she began to juggle her commitment to her husband and the anticipated excitement of the new relationship. The "cloud of sexual excitement," as she referred to this thoughtform, was moving in and out all the time they were together.

During one of these meetings when talking about obsessions, Y. told her that on more than one occasion he had experienced uncontrollable attacks of lust. Once, in the middle of a spiritual gathering, the lady with whom he was dining had to run away in panic, while the people at the other tables were shocked by his strange behavior. The man also told her about his past in the drug world. (Note: The use of strong "recreational" drugs might leave the auric field exposed to many kinds of collective thoughtforms.) From the beginning of the relationship with Y. she began seeing her husband in a new light (or, shall we say, shadow). In a period of days the things she didn't like in her husband were magnified to such an extreme that the idea her marriage was a failure gripped her mind. She was able to fight this idea with logic; but, when Mr. Y. repeatedly appeared in her dreams to reinforce the negative information about her husband, it became too much for her to handle on her own.

At the time she talked with me, she told me that although she was falling in love with Y., she knew that there was no possible future with him, the two of them being so dissimilar in life objectives. On the other hand, her perception of her husband had changed so much that it was difficult to feel love anymore. Her husband now represented all the tyrannical, dry, masculine force in the universe. She felt justified in exploring other relationships in order to recover part of her freedom. Still, the main commitment of this woman was to her spiritual path in the form of service to others, a work she knew would be fulfilled much better with her husband's help.

Upon opening up my clairvoyance, I perceived several dirty purple-reddish tentacles attached to the sexual area, the abdominal region, and the neck of H. Following the tentacles, I saw a reddish-purple cloud about the size of a city that extended toward the town where the man lived, although I had no sense of orientation at the time of my search. This cloud was definitively evil and alive with millions of thoughts such as "Everybody is perverted and selfish, so I'll live life for my own benefit...Immediate satisfaction is all that life is about...I might play the victim, but I will suck as much as I can from those around me."

This cloud or macro-thoughtform was permanently hooked to Y., as well as it is to thousands of others around the world. It was powerful enough to create definite physical sensations and overshadow H.'s thoughts with its own set of negative perceptions. The macro-thoughtform was using Y. as an instrument to affect H.'s life. At the time of therapy I cut the tentacles of the psychic monster attached to H.

We also had to deal with another extension of the macro-thoughtform. This one I perceived in the form of a little purplish, distorted fetus, making mockery of everything, located just inside the uterus of H. I was unaware of it until she complained about a recent bladder irritation. We concluded that this thoughtform was the arrow of energy she felt coming from Y.'s second chakra the first time she met him. At the time the parasite was implanted, it manipulated H.'s sensations around that area and even her thoughts in order to recharge itself every time she acted alone upon her sexual fantasies with Y.

By clearing H. of the influence of these etheric creatures, her perception changed. Y. lost all appeal to her in an instant, and her husband was no longer the "bad guy."

She stopped seeing Y. and kept a close watch over her thoughts for the next month until all thoughts about failure in her marriage disappeared. The dreams she was having with Y. stopped. She also spoke with her husband about some changes she would like to see in the relationship, and everything ended well.

Although Mrs. H. is a sensitive, intelligent, and spiritually oriented person, it was still impossible for her to perceive the subtle manipulation of her mind and bodily sensations caused by this ancestral thoughtform. Cases such as this sound bizarre, but one wonders how many marriages end in divorce because of the upheaval produced by these ancient malefic clouds.

We are immersed in an ocean of thoughtforms. I have only described one such dramatic case, but there are innumerable macro-thoughtforms created by the whole field of our life's experience that limit us in ways we are not always aware of. For example, most human beings believe they have to pay with work or suffering for what they receive from life; that they can't be happy if certain conditions are not met; that they can't survive if certain conditions are not provided, etc. These are a few macro-thoughtforms our culture has accepted as laws of nature. Although there have been rare cases demonstrating that these commonly held beliefs are not immutable rules, we still consider them law. Thoughtforms veil or prevent the clear manifestation of the spiritual self on earth. Our task is to remove as many veils as we are aware of in order to expand our awareness and experience life as close to perfection as possible.

After I gave a lecture on thoughtforms in Boston, a girl from the audience requested an appointment. As soon as she crossed the door of my temporary office the next day I felt an overwhelming sexual attraction to her. An inner certainty came to me: I only needed to act on my instinctual urgency and she would yield immediately. No words would be necessary. I recognized she was pretty, but my reaction was out of proportion, even if she were a centerfold!

As soon as I looked for the cause of my reaction I saw a thoughtform the size of a king-sized bed floating over her head; a tentacle the width of an arm was hooked into her sexual area; other tentacles were coming at me.

We sat and I talked first, telling her about this blind force in her aura. She told me this was the reason for her visit—the thoughtform had been affixed to her after a torrid relation with an unfaithful metaphysician who tried to keep her and another woman at the same time. My patient left him, but he told her, in a very deep and mysterious voice, that she would never forget him. Since that conversation she was obsessed with erotic fantasies of every kind; she had been unable to experience romance afterwards because all men reacted toward her the same way I felt, usually with less control.

The girl was certain the metaphysician was still projecting his evil influence over her, but I saw that, although the thoughtform came from this man during sexual intercourse, it was an independent creature by now. She had nourished the thoughtform unconsciously with her paranoid-victim feelings.

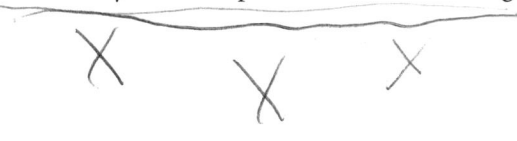

After disintegrating the thoughtform I was able to see her as a normal human being; then I gave her instructions on how to prevent its future reconfiguration.

These stories raise questions about how to know when sexual attraction is a natural response to energy affinity and when it is based on influences of a lower order. I don't think there is an easy answer. The possibility of correctly evaluating magnetic attraction only appears after the feelings have been purified in a long initiatory process. Then the feelings are responsive to one's intuition, to the higher archetypal currents, and not to the repressions and consequent overcompensations each personality suffers in the everyday world. Thus, I will illustrate with the following story of another case of sexuality, but one following a higher archetypal pattern.

In one of my meditations I invoked Osiris, the god of eternal life. In the middle of it I suddenly felt my face taking the form of a ram. I felt horns over my head and a curiously fiery, intensely masculine energy not normally considered part of the spectrum of sensations related to Osiris's energy. I felt a transpersonal presence inside me. He told me he was Knemu. I recognized the name as that of an obscure god of the Egyptian pantheon of whom I knew nothing.

"I need you to do work for me. Would you like to help me?" he said.

"What do you want me to do for you?" I answered.

Knemu responded, "You will know soon."

In this realm I go by feeling the energy of the being; its energy was crisp and pure. Since I trusted my feelings, I accepted. I nearly felt pity for this almost-forgotten spiritual entity without a priest to represent him on earth in our times.

That same afternoon a woman of twenty-six years, blonde, and with an innocent girlish face came to talk with me. She had been my student in the past. Now everything was fine in her life. . .except that it took a lot of courage for her to ask me, and very indirectly, if I was willing to be her first man.

It was after a few days that I had access to the books on Egyptian mythology that mention Knemu. There I learned that he was worshipped in the spring when virgins were taken to the temples to be deflowered by the priests in the renewal celebrations of nature. . . Yes, it was spring, too.

At certain times I have seen things that resemble thought-forms but feel alien, of independent origin, devoid of emotional or conceptual frequencies that usually characterize human creations. I perceive their lifeforce as primitive as that of a virus, a ruthless drive to absorb energy to exist at all cost. I was the host of several of these creatures once. It happened when I superimposed two very powerful exercises to raise kundalini from different traditions, but it had a shattering effect on me. I felt as if I were in a rocket going to the remotest galaxy, and when I came back I saw my aura full of strange black-and-white worm-shaped creatures. They were about a foot long, giving off a pure high-frequency electrical force and moving in my auric field like eels.

I had never seen anything like it and did not know what to think about them. But the feeling was definitely bad, so I tried to clear them from my aura. After twenty minutes of purification exercises, four or five of these creatures still remained with me. I didn't force them out anymore, but waited to see what their effect was in real life.

It was a big mistake. I developed a strange mouth infection that had to be treated by professionals. They took all sorts of cultures, but never could find if it had been caused by a virus, a germ, a bacterium, or God knows what. My energy was nearly all drained and I could do very little to fight back magically. It took me almost forty days to recover.

Another case involving a weird creature of this same nature happened to a student of mine. This lady called me after three days of a continuous headache. Her mind was continuously out of focus and she was completely devitalized. It all started when she received a demonstration of energy from a psychic friend of hers. The man said he had received the energy from a telepathic contact with extraterrestrials and for a few minutes laid his hands over her head.

When I met with her I saw something that resembled a legless black-widow spider with an almost-spherical shiny black body and a tiny head, its small mouth attached tenaciously to my student's cerebellum. Upon removing the little etheric vampire, she recovered in twenty-four hours.

Not everything in my work is this horrible. I have also had very gratifying experiences working with serious students of other spiritual disciplines. When doing energy work on these people I have felt their spiritual teachers' presences working through my aura to boost the session's effect on their students.

At least on three occasions I have seen my hair turn into an Afro; I looked at my feet and they were bare, my body covered by an orange robe. It was then that I realized the presence of the most-famous guru in India was synergizing my work. When I was done, I saw tears on my students' faces. And when I asked them if they were devotees of Sai Baba, they answered: "Yes, and it felt as if I were in his ashram. I know he was here."

This same type of experience has happened with Paramhansa Yogananda, the founder of the Self Realization Fellowship based in California. One time in San Francisco I saw the presence of Bagawan Rajneesh in the corner of the hotel room. This was not a big surprise because I knew the student I was working with to be a disciple of the controversial guru who had been expelled from several countries. I had not read anything about this guru, so it took me some time to dare tell my student, "This is embarrassing, but your guru wants me to tell you that your aura is full of shit, and that you should laugh about it." I never knew if this was either a joke or an obscure part of Rajneesh philosophy, but our student jumped up in happiness exclaiming, "Yes! Yes! That's my guru!"

I saw the presence of Swami Muktananda, the founder of the Siddha Yoga tradition in America, before I knew how he looked. By his subtle body he helped correct imbalances in my own energy channels. Months later I saw his face on a book cover. His own guru, Nitiyananda, once worked through me when I was with a Siddha Yoga practitioner. My energy beams were magnified impressively, and the body of my student arched, the back of his head touching his back. He became all rigid and very hot. He slid from the chair onto the floor, seeing light all around, and exclaiming, "I have read about this in books. Wow! Do you have a video camera?" He was exhibiting some of the classic symptoms of kundalini rising.

On two occasions I have seen spiritual guardians on the invisible planes checking me out before I was allowed to lay my hands on their protégées. The first time it happened I was in Marbella, Spain. A beautiful dark-skinned woman of intense magnetism came before the audience to receive a demonstration of my energies. I put my hands over her head, closed my eyes, and saw three stern black men around me. They were in a mist of power and mystery, looking deep into my being. It was scary due to their sudden apparition in the middle of the stressful social situation I was working.

Politely, I requested permission to do my energy work and expanded my heart chakra as a symbol of fraternity. They moved out a few steps. As I performed my public demonstration the woman entered into a deep trance. It took her a few minutes to recover after my part was done.

She told me later she was a Tuareg princess and a priestess of this North African nomadic desert tribe. She was a magician in her own right and was protected in the spiritual realms by generations of powerful shamans who had taken care of her bloodline since remote times.

Something similar happened when I demonstrated the STAR*LIFE energies to a witch, a high priestess of the Druidic tradition. I saw four mysterious non-human entities making certain I was not going to mess up the woman's aura. She later confirmed that she had established astral relationships with four animal spirits to protect her in case of need.

Not all the relationships between humans and spirits are this positive. I remember a sequence of events that shows the reality—and negativity—of one of these invisible beings named "Gray Wolf." I realize that several people in the Native American Indian community might have used, or still use, the name "Gray Wolf." I am not making reference to any specific individual, merely pointing out a series of striking events relating only to this name.

My story begins in Connecticut in the house of a charming and gifted artist, healer, psychic, and speaker who organized a talk and presentation of STAR*LIFE. All the attendants were in their seats when I came into the room. The moment I started talking I noticed a strong blockage in between my thoughts and their verbalization—as if they were being held above me so that I had to force their way through my head. This might happen to me the first few minutes of a talk, but that night the delay between sentences was longer than usual, and it didn't disappear in the warmth of my exposition.

While giving the lecture, a part of my mind was still involved in looking for the cause of this problem, and it directed my attention to a robust, dark-skinned man sitting in the remotest corner spot. He had long hair and a disturbing energy field. Another part of me felt embarrassed for differentiating the American Indian from the rest of the audience. But my mistrust proved to be correct during the second half of the lecture when the man, using English in a very clever way, asked me almost unintelligible questions preceded by elaborate sophisms subtly used to denigrate the information I was providing that night.

We engaged in a short philosophical battle which resulted in my favor, although I do not know how. At the end of the lecture the man introduced himself to me as a full-blooded shaman from the wolf clan, who had been on the road with the most-important contemporary figures of the American Indian spiritual movement. He said that he was destined to be as great as his old friends, but he had strayed off his assigned path and now was unable to find his way back into the light. He told me about tragic things that happened in his youth. I did not realize at the time that this was his strategy to stimulate my compassion as an energy link. Finally, humbly, he asked me for any guidance on how to reconnect with his spirit.

I saw an etheric opening in his back like a wound between his shoulder blades. I felt that the opening was a hereditary feature used by the transpersonal entities of his tribe to work through the man, to come into his body in mediumistic work. I told him this opening could prove positive only within the context of an Indian's life, but it was a dangerous opening for lower psychic entities living in a white man's civilization. I recommended to him that he close this gap to avoid being swept by passions and vices.

He criticized my advice, not only telling me that my perception was incorrect, but also that he was strong enough to protect himself under any circumstances. We talked for almost twenty minutes. During the whole conversation he tried to get information involving my procedures for handling power by using symbols. At the end of the conversation I was very tired.

My bedroom for the night was next to the lecture room. Although I was exhausted, in my final reveries before sinking into sleep I saw something that made me jump out of bed. A dark curtain of fog about four yards in height and two-hundred yards in width was circling the house. It was coming to steal my power. Under any other circumstance I would have felt that this evil emanation was only a part of my shadow, manifesting in my personal life as a series of denied or unassimilated events. My strategy then would have been to embrace it and make it merge with my universal self where no power could escape me because I can contain all there is. But this was a different story. The fog was overwhelmingly powerful, lurking in the woods out there, waiting for me to fall completely asleep when it would sever my link with my Higher Self. I knew it was connected to the shaman. I did a banishing ritual in my bedroom and the thing went away, but my sleep was restless that night.

The next morning a synchronous event I experienced made me realize the challenge of the Indian was not over. A friend from the house gave me an old Indian head/buffalo nickel! Later, on my way out of town, I found one of my hands bleeding. I still want to believe I cut my hand inadvertently while carrying my luggage rushing to the train station. But two things were out of order: most of the time I had my gloves on since it was mid-January; and, although the cut was superficial, it had taken away my skin in the perfect form of an Indian arrowhead! I still have the scar.

The train took me to Hanover, New Hampshire. There I gave another lecture where a lady with clearly American Indian features unsuccessfully maneuvered to make me feel uncomfortable about the STAR*LIFE prices. At the end she decided to have a private session with me.

The day of the session I saw a sinuous evil fog above her crown chakra. I asked if she was engaged in mediumistic or channeling practices. After she acknowledged this I asked her about the quality of her contacts. That was when she told me of her concerns over a psychic entity appearing in her meditations and dreams. His name was Gray Wolf, and during one dream he had taken her eyes out and replaced them with his own. He promised her power if she would follow his instructions.

I warned her about the potential evil hanging over her head; power was her obsession due to a very difficult beginning in life, but it was not the solution. Power without love would certainly unbalance her life.

The coincidence of the meeting with the shaman from the wolf clan and its negative consequences and the name of the evil spirit did not go unnoticed by me. My next town on the tour was Burlington, Vermont. There at a dinner conversation I related the story to a group of friends.

In the group that night was a highly spiritual woman who was intuitively attuned to the shamanistic path. She did powerful healings using feathers and other traditional elements. She said that over the years she had heard the name "Gray Wolf" twice— both times it had been a spirit who had promised power to its victims, then distorted their auras to the point where their lives became miserable, even tragic.

I did not mention the story again until almost a year later in Houston, Texas at a lunch with distant relatives. An old man, husband of my mother's cousin, told me his father had a confrontation in the Twenties with a real shaman called "Gray Wolf."

My relative's dad used to have a good relationship with the Indians of a neighboring reservation in Colorado until he noticed chickens disappearing from his farm. Blaming the Indians for the thievery, he took his horse and rifle and galloped across an Indian ceremony. Gray Wolf, the shaman of the tribe, swore he would avenge the profanation. Nothing happened to the old man, but... it is difficult not to think there might be a mysterious connection between these events.

Now with my thoughts on the American Indian tradition, I would like to share another curious story that happened in San Clemente, California.

Sometimes on my trips to Los Angeles I used to stay overnight in the spacious healing office of a friend who collected Native American Indian art. One night when I was in my sleeping bag, I began to see hypnagogic images in the form of designs similar to Navajo sand paintings. After a few minutes the colors changed predominantly to oranges and reds; then the angles became acute, menacing. Finally, I felt a challenging presence trying to scare me out of the house. Because I was tired and wanted to sleep, I first tried to engage in telepathic communication with the entity. But the energy patterns were becoming more and more violent. I warned the entity it was going to get in trouble by messing with me. My bragging didn't stop it. Then I stood up and in a very bad mood made a ritual clearing. After this the psychic atmosphere was pure again so I returned to my sleeping bag.

Just before falling asleep I saw a very tall Indian with an exceptionally strong naked torso cautiously approaching me. He was the one creating the aggressive patterns before; now he was requesting my permission to visit my friend in the house—he was looking for romance. I said to the Indian that it was none of my business what they wanted to do together; I was not going to interfere. Then I saw him disappearing into the main house.

I would have forgotten the whole incident if it were not for my friend's comments the next morning.

"I feel beaten," she complained. "This was one of those nights."

"Didn't you sleep well?"

"Not really. This has happened to me before. I dreamed that I danced in the mountains all night with an Indian; I had rattles [Indian bells] on my legs, but still they didn't protect me from the thorny bushes, and now my legs hurt. I feel as if it really happened."

"I can't believe it! I saw an Indian trying to come to you last night!"

"Oh, really? How did he look?"

My description matched hers perfectly. Then she showed me her ankles and lower legs. She had bruises that were not there the night before.

To my knowledge it never happened again. On my next trips I used to tease her, moving my body as a cowboy, ready to draw his pistols: "Don't worry, babe. Everything's gonna be all right. I'll protect you from the Indians tonight!"

Some people are not linked with spirits but with archetypes. I know an enlightened Ph.D. in Texas who is using her prominent social position to work for the soul of the city of Dallas. Her aim is to link the subconscious of the people with the symbol of an archetype that can better the destiny of the whole city. At the time of her Cosmic Activation I contacted two Greek powers working through her, Pegasus and Athena. She, being a magician of a social order, was aware of them, too.

I have met several individuals whose souls were linked to the Christ consciousness. For many years I have been contacted by what I call the "Cosmic Christ," a conscious frequency of love, life, righteousness, and order I see in a golden light all around the planet now. I think this is the return of the Christ many talk about, but I doubt whether He is coming through a single spiritual leader in our times. Instead, I know that the Christ consciousness is expressing its multidimensional influence through the souls of diverse individuals. I have met about four of them, but I know there are thousands out there. Their distinctive note is a feeling of fraternity and an intuitive recognition of the sacredness of life, although in young Christbearers this vibration may manifest as idealist messianic tendencies.

Some others have to deal with transcendent powers of a dispersive nature. I encountered this at the time of a telepathic Cosmic Activation when my new client and I, being in different cities, synchronized our meditations as I moved in the spirit to perform the Cosmic Activation where he was. I saw a gigantic demon torturing him, taking him to hells of anguish and suffering. It took me a lot of time to pass through its influence and do my work. When I was finished, I still felt the demon around. I knew it would return, but at the same time I felt that the pure energy of my student would create a climate of understanding and integration very beneficial for future development of that strange relation.

When I talked with the man over the phone and described as softly as I could my vision and what it meant, he let me know the cause of all this. He identified the demonic being at once: he had been diagnosed with AIDS four-and-a-half years before.

At times I have met souls with frequencies very different from those of regular human beings. I discover this difference when I focus clairvoyantly on the causal body. The causal body is perceived on a subjective level of awareness—outside time and space. This is why the few clairvoyants who see it describe it in a variety of ways. For purposes of diagnosis I see it as a sphere of about nine yards in diameter surrounding the physical body. I can see it in other ways, too, but this model allows me to draw more-practical information for my students.

The causal body is the vehicle of the Soul and contains the grooves of consciousness, the source of everything that happens to us in this lifetime. These grooves, according to Hindu cosmology, are created by experiences previous to birth.

Reading the causal body brings information about what we might call, for lack of a better theoretical model, past lives or states of existence. Reading the causal body is also helpful in understanding the level of spiritual evolution correlated to the degree of love, wisdom, and power radiated from the individual Soul when coming into the physical world.

In reading the causal body I have become aware of the basic differences between individuals. Some of them really stand out from the norm; their causal matrix emanates qualities not found in regular human beings. The most-common difference is an addition of extraterrestrial frequencies I can see coming through those who have a cone of indigo color, mentioned at the beginning of this chapter. The extraterrestrial energy comes down and expands in the causal body as an indigo field speckled with silver like the night sky.

People with this frequency all share a longing to "go home"; most of them are not well adapted to life on this planet. Their sensitive spirits resent the coarseness in which they live, and usually they express feelings as criticism, sarcasm, and alienation. Some of them feel lost, ungrounded, or unable to identify with regular human interests which involve career, family, or sensorial gratification.

A few feel they are here for a purpose; they anxiously look through books and seminars on spiritual, occult, or metaphysical subjects. All seem to have a reason to be here because they are part of an inconceivable stream of consciousness and energy sent to our planet from a remote system. They are the individual cells of a formless entity transforming our whole civilization by the transference of these units of consciousness into human bodies.

It is a lonely, painful mission, especially when they don't know about it. Fortunately, many of those awakening are forming associations with other star-people, but there is also a negative aspect to this recognition of difference, that is, such elitism gives them a sense of separation not conducive to fully integrating with life on this planet. They are in dire need of developing their love of physical existence, for only then will they be able to bring forth the great power of their cosmic heritage.

There are others, more rarely encountered in my work, who possess an angelic essence. In these angelic souls I see a rosy blissful radiance of universal love coming from their causal bodies. They are ethereal; they bring ecstasy wherever they go. I love working with them!

I have seen one fallen angel, too—the soul of a psychologist, president of a prestigious esoteric organization. The revelation of his true nature was most startling to me since I had been living in his house for three days and we had formed a great friendship. A short, soft, friendly man, a perfect gentleman of deep philosophical mind and serious involvement with human welfare, he was especially interested in the archetypal currents behind the Judaic, Christian, and Islamic traditions.

At the time of this causal body reading I discovered something I can describe only as a devil—I saw this being looking directly at me as a mighty, ruthless rebel. It was cold, unapproachable. The vibration was so coarse that the causal body of my host looked like pieces of obsidian stone, all black and sharp and dangerous. He seemed to have a very heavy karma to deal with and an unimaginable power kept under very tight self-control.

"Do you feel as if you have a great power that can very easily be used for destruction?" I asked. "Do you feel you are expiating some kind of heavy crime from the past, related to abuse of power?" I continued. My friend answered that he was aware of all this. He knew he was different; he remembered a previous life in Atlantis where he had been responsible for vast destruction. He had been coming back to earth to learn how to love.

Other causal bodies also have a non-human feeling, but they seem to belong to a parallel line of evolution. I relate their vibration to diverse kinds of nature spirits. Most of these people are hypersensitive and demonstrate an impermanence in their emotions, their lifestyles, their relationships, their work. They are bohemian, wonderful to be around—for awhile.

One nature spirit I encountered was different in its rank as well as in its physical manifestation. This happened in the house of an alternative-healing teacher. One of her students was a strong, beautiful woman in her late thirties. Her son, whom she brought to me for an Activation, was in her arms. He was eleven-years old, though the size of a five-year old. His limbs were without flesh; his eyes moved aimlessly at the phantom commands of a dead brain.

She wanted me to explore the possibility of connecting a little more of his spirit—if he had one left—to his body. We went into the healing room with two other women and I did my best to connect his root chakra to the earth. Since the chakra had a cottony feeling, my energy was going through it without causing any effect, like wind through a fluffy net. I forced myself to create a change for about five minutes, but to no avail.

Then I looked for the spirit above, my aim being to persuade him to descend into the physical dimension to accept the reality of a crippled body and live out the experience fully. To my surprise as I was lifting my psychic sight to find the spirit, I saw a magnificent rainbow-colored funnel of energy about the size of a tornado. It was the real soul of the child's body; it emanated a sparkling, joyous quality in full contrast to the feelings that the sight of his physical self elicited in humans. I got goose bumps. The energy itself descended into the room and the three women there, without knowing why, started crying tears of happiness.

"Fool!" the magnificent nature being spoke to me, "How could you imagine I would descend from this freedom at your request? Do you think the little creature is wrong in not having a mind? Some of us choose to work from up here. I created this little piece of flesh for the woman to recognize me. We have an old, very old link. Once she learns to find me as I really am, I will drop the body and will work through her in diverse modalities of energy healing she does not even dream about now... I have set the whole scenario for the woman to be free from economic worries, fully focused on healing for the last ten years, and now I am just waiting for her sensitivity to develop. Let her know about all this!"

There was almost no need for words; the three women knew a holy presence had been in the room. They believed everything I said. The mother told me the doctor who delivered the baby damaged his brain; after they sued him they got enough to live on comfortably. She had indeed been looking for alternative systems of healing and in search of something that could be useful for the boy. She knew he was going to die soon, and she knew she was called to do healing for others in the future. However, she did not understand how this could happen. It was a bittersweet emotional experience for all of us involved!

9

NAVIGATING THROUGH FEAR

Most spiritual seekers today are willing to take years of humiliation from old-fashioned gurus, mortify their flesh through diets and ascetic disciplines, plug themselves into every new brain machine on the market, spend thousands on metaphysical seminars, repeat decrees, mantrams, or positive affirmations like zombies, spend hours without end in sitting meditation, hit the bed and yell incoherences to empty chairs. But they are afraid of magic mushrooms because they know once swallowed, they cannot stop them. It is the real, primitive, original method of transcendence. Unfortunately, too much of the real thing!

People in the enlightenment game often want to remain on campus with their other fellow students. Nobody is really looking forward to graduation because that means real work is coming their way. In this light, New Age organizations are no more than social clubs with metaphysical philosophies. At least Rotarians and Christian fraternities help the community!

The institutions which emphasize transcendence offer the newcomer a wide variety of beliefs. Some believe the space brothers are coming to take them out of trouble, or that they are part of them. Some believe in salvation after being good, or *Satori* after a hundred seshins, or *samadhi* after a few-hundred-thousand mantrams, or Nirvana after a few-hundred incarnations. Some believe in Jesus Christ, or the words of wisdom from their favorite channel, or the shakti of their guru, or in Amen, Om, Hare Krishna, Ham-sa, or "Namiojo renge kio"! But...what is behind all these institutionalized beliefs? What are they really doing with all this mental juggling and with all this pinkish light of "unconditional love"? I think most of the individuals involved are really hiding from the responsibility of being themselves. They like to remain disciples, followers, admirers—sheep for the rest of their lives.

Of course, everyone has to start somewhere. But often the motivation for enlightenment degenerates with time. They might have started with enthusiasm and practiced the disciplines with stern determination in the beginning, but after awhile they become accustomed to the idea that they are on a never-ending quest. Everybody in the group keeps telling them that real enlightenment consists of enjoying the road as much as the destination, so they relax. Now they have a few friends who think alike, and everybody gets enough self-esteem from feeling they belong to an exclusive elite pursuing higher goals, and enough thrill from the lectures, books, and seminars they consume. After all, they think, the spiritual path is but a pleasant journey through the eternal spiral of time.

Watch out! Don't let the fiery spirit of your youth die out in social or "holy" routines! Self-complacency is a friend in times of crisis, but a subtle enemy in times of peace. I'm not proposing the cultivation of anxiety to achieve the rewards of enlightenment.

I am pointing to a higher joy through a way of life that keeps you young and vibrant—not by diets and energizing pills, but by living to the fullest. And this only happens if you dare to challenge your limitations again and again.

"But what about the children?" you say, "those innocent souls who do not deserve to suffer just because I become an eccentric." Children today need to be exposed to change. Since it is a continuous condition of our times, we need to learn to live with it. Children crave change, stimulus, yearn for wonders. It is the "mature" adults who overprotect and transfer their own anxieties over to them. As long as a parent is with them and they understand the rules of the new game, they feel safe.

Luisa and I tell our children about everything. They understand the most-abstract metaphysical concepts and are not afraid, but proud, of being different. They know others do not understand our views. They have learned to be respectful of their friend's ideologies, yet centered on their own.

When I was sixteen, I began my path in the ascetic disciplines of Hatha yoga. I entered a very strict organization in México City. We were not allowed to have meat, chicken, fish, coffee, cigarettes, or any alcoholic beverage, including champagne. The "Great Guru" founder of this organization once expelled a disciple who was caught eating beans fried in pork fat, the most common dish in México.

For ten years I strictly followed the rules of this organization, practicing Hatha yoga and meditation every day. By the time I was twenty-four I moved back to Tijuana, México. There I became the director of the school of astrology and the college of instructors of Hatha yoga.

One day when I was practicing my disciplines I heard a voice telling me I should stop doing Hatha yoga. It didn't make sense to me since I was at that time a fanatic of perseverance. But the voice was correct; it warned me about what finally happened because I didn't act upon the message. A motorcycle-jumping excursion followed by an intense session of Hatha yoga damaged my back and made it very difficult for me to achieve the yogic contortions I was used to. One year later I resigned from this sect, not due to any problems with yoga, but as a result of a discussion with the "Great Guru."

He was a man with a terrific voice, intense and commanding eyes framed by long white hair and a beard. He always wore a white shirt and pants, sandals and a white cape that gave him the look of a high-ranking templar knight. The great guru had a great heart, a dictatorial attitude, and a most powerful aura, by which he produced at times by his mere presence, interesting atmospheric phenomena. He wanted to change the world by impressing others outside with the cleanliness of the lifestyle he proposed, so he demanded all his students act and look like boy scouts. Under his vision thousands aligned. They opened yoga institutes, vegetarian restaurants, nutrition stores, and masonic lodges all over south and central America.

One day I told him about my interest in magic. He answered: "Don't fool yourself. There are no higher beings. Your work is here, with the institution. This is all the magic there is. . ." It was clearly my time to move out.

I studied magic mostly on my own, but I had the encouragement and support of two graduates from a magical order that prospered during the Sixties and Seventies in the Mojave Desert, north of Los Angeles. In 1980 they showed me the basic movements of ritual and disclosed to me the precise techniques of the highest secret of their organization: sexual magic.

One day one of my teachers of magic came through Tijuana to invite me to a magical encampment. He was heading south with two Germans. I joined the passengers in the land-rover and we cruised away looking for adventure.

On the road my teacher introduced me to the Germans. The old man had a mischievous smile, eyes that receded whenever you looked into them, and big, broad, short, primitive, dangerous hands. He was an ex-officer of the SS still on a mission: to take care of one of the children of Hitler, one of the many Hitler begat to make certain his genetic line would survive and have a chance at world power if he ever failed.

You can imagine who the other German was—a man of breathtaking beauty, a true Teutonic god with long golden hair, medium height, but a perfectly proportioned hero's body. He had been trained all his life to be what he was: a superb athlete, a black belt, a genius in matters of strategy and war. He was the incarnation of Thor. He was in his thirties but looked twenty-six. He had a mission, too; he was going to learn magic, talk to his Guardian Angel, ask for its help to find the Holy Grail, and then steal the Holy Spear and conquer the world!

They had three plans to achieve world recognition:

1. They had lists of ex-Nazi officers living in South American countries. It was only a matter of getting their money by extorting their patriotic ideals or their fear of being exposed to the international committee for the investigation of war crimes.

2. They planned to participate in and win the future Olympics, then start their own political campaign.

3. They possessed a book called *The Magical Diary of Hitler*, supposedly a compilation of Hitler's personal notes. They had the typed manuscripts and were about to look for a publisher. The manuscript was in the car and they asked my opinion. They were especially interested in my reaction to the section where Hitler describes his initiation into a circle of exotic personalities, including Master Morya. The initiation was to help him come to terms with his world mission. In it he was ritualistically treated as Jacques de Molay, the last of the Templar masters, by the Holy Inquisition. After torture, he then was buried alive in a big sarcophagus where he had sex with a virgin, then killed her with his own hands.

I wasn't impressed. I had previously read the essence of that ceremony and could see that the book was a fake. It had dramatized, well-interwoven versions of information coming from the books of Castaneda, Alice Bailey, and Anton Szandor LaVey, among others.

With my suspicions piqued, it now was time for me to check them out. "Why is it important for you to get the Holy Grail?" I asked.

The conqueror-to-be answered, "The Holy Grail and the Holy Spear are talismans of world power activated by those with a certain genetic code—my own. My father only got the spear, but if I get the two of them, nobody will be able to stop me."

"Are you still into killing all the Jews?" was my next question.

"No, our war is against the multinationals who erode individualized consciousness. We are not against the race; behind the multinational corporations there are Jews in spirit but they may or may not be of Jewish blood. Those are the ones we want to exterminate."

"Are you willing to use violence to do this?" I added.

"Well," Hitler's son answered, "I have been trained in all tactics. You give me any weapon in total darkness and I know how to operate it instantly. But most of the time you don't have to use violence. It's just a matter of kidnapping the families of those you need to persuade. You don't do anything to them or to their families, but you always get what you want."

"Did you know that the whole tradition and technique of contacting the Guardian Angel is of Jewish origin?" I asked.

"Yes, I know. That's why I am learning magic—to find a non-Kabalistic, non-Jewish method to accomplish that."

Maybe they were crazy, I thought, but I was only twenty-five at the time, and even the prospect of a bad adventure with them was better than no adventure at all.

We drove to Ensenada and stayed for a few hours in the house of an old friend of mine. She was a mature woman who was a psychic, astrologer, and ex-yoga teacher, a rich and refined woman living in a beautiful house over a mountain with a magnificent view of the bay. There I had the opportunity to see the warrior god's horoscope. It showed a genial mind with no grounding at all, an incurable egotist.

In Ensenada after we joined with my second teacher of magic, we then drove to the mountains to establish our encampment. The whole trip had been organized by my first teacher to test Hitler's son's magical abilities.

At night we built a fire. My teacher and his new pupil practiced advanced black-belt exercises for awhile. Later the first magician asked his apprentice to draw a magical circle of about thirty yards for protection. Since this included our vehicles, Hitler's son answered, "I do not know if I can build a circle that big." He worked on the ritualistic procedure and after five minutes returned to us saying, "There is something very wicked out there." I got goose bumps instantly, together with a full state of alertness. I scanned with my Third Eye the peaceful valley we were in, looking for the enemy, but I couldn't perceive anything. Could it be that my psychic senses were not keen enough to find the evil lurking in the shadows?

We did an invocation to Thoth, the god of magic of the ancient Egyptians. Then our teacher took his new disciple away. When they returned we all slipped into our sleeping bags.

I slept for about two hours, then woke up suddenly. Our fire was almost dead. The Germans were in their sleeping bags, but the magicians were gone. When I stood up I saw a fire spark in the bushes about one-hundred yards outside our circle.

Still cautious of the possibility of a wicked entity, I walked in that direction. I had seen the flash of the cigarette lighter at the right moment; my teachers were there, talking.

"What do you think about them?" the first magician asked abruptly when he saw me approaching.

"The book's a fake and the horoscope says he is not going to make it. Besides, I don't know about the wickedness he saw outside," I answered.

My teacher then said, "The wickedness was there, inside him. But something else made me realize he is not ready for further training: I offered to guide him on an LSD journey to accelerate his contact with his Guardian Angel, but he refused. He said his path was that of no drugs. He was not ready to deal with his darkness yet."

That was a complete shock to me. I didn't know my teacher used hallucinogenics in his training. I didn't know that what I considered the hallmark of spirituality—the pride of doing everything out of my own self without external influences—was for him cowardice disguised as self-righteousness. Moreover, he had never offered LSD to me and I had been studying with him for more than a year while the other guy was just a newcomer! And there was also the weird sensation that I knew my teacher knew I would have answered the same if he had ever offered me the LSD trip!

Since then I have studied everything I could about mind-altering drugs. I became interested in natural substances such as peyote and mushrooms. I learned that they are not addictive and are still an integral part of sacred ceremonies of prehispanic origin.

The Germans disappeared from our lives, thank God! They never found a publisher for their collection of weirdness. Hitler's son didn't even qualify for the Olympics; he was too old already. They may be in South America by now blackmailing decrepit WWII criminals. Who knows?

My first actual experience with a mind-altering substance was with hashish. My teacher told me it was softer than other substances and would prepare the way without shocking my system.

That night he asked me to remain relaxed and with my eyes closed. Suddenly I was taken out of my body into celestial regions; feelings of unutterable purity went through my ethereal body. Then, I descended softly, like a leaf in autumn. When I recovered and told him about my experience, he explained how by an act of will he was able to transfer his energy temporarily to lift me up to a more-refined transpersonal level. I didn't like the idea that I had to depend on him to reach those heights. I then tried to repeat the experience on my own, but unsuccessfully.

He also showed me how to use the hands for scanning diverse energies. He put several Tarot cards face down on the table and asked me to discover by feel the one more akin to my nature. He demonstrated how to move the hands over the table, eight inches over the cards. It was amazing for me to see how my hand plunged dramatically, like a very strong magnet, towards a specific card whenever it was over it. After turning the card over we put it back with the others, shuffled the group, and placed them once again out on the table. That night, with the help of hashish, I was able to pick the same card four times.

His last instruction that night involved a psychic procedure to extract information from unknown symbols such as the strange hieroglyphs from ancient cultures. He drew a symbol unknown to me and asked me to rise to the transpersonal levels on my own until I found a door with that symbol engraved on it. Then I should open the door and describe what I see on its other side.

I saw a skull, then a bridge of gold over an abyss of blackness. The bridge of gold ended on a golden sphere. After I described my vision, he said it was accurate since the symbol was used in a templar secret ritual of death and resurrection.

Later I did experiments with cannabis, always in my temple, inside my magical circle, after ceremonial invocations. I never felt satisfied with its results. It never helped me pierce any veil of consciousness, but only expanded and combined what was already in my mind. I abandoned it quickly.

My clairvoyance and my highest achievements in mysticism are not dependent on drugs of any kind. I have never gotten drunk; I have only smoked in ceremonial settings. I have never used cocaine, narcotics, or any other artificial mind-altering drugs. I don't have an addictive personality. That is why I can look people in the eye and talk about my findings with full honesty.

I have worked with every technique, old and modern, to expand the mind—from seclusion, fast, and prayer to the most bizarre practices in heterosexual magic—and I believe magic mushrooms, used properly, are the quickest way to unlock a human being's potential.

There are many teachers who can tell me how to be a better human being, and many who can show me a new road to the same old mountain, perhaps even a different tradition or a new technology. But for years I have tried unsuccessfully to find a teacher in the flesh who still has something for me to learn on the road to higher evolution. Now my only guides are Life, my inner contacts, my spiritual self. And, in México, the power who manifests through the magic mushrooms.

When using mushrooms I'm not looking for a high or bliss. Every experience is a sacred voyage to meet a most-wondrous entity, a multidimensional being I can't even begin to describe. It is warm and affectionate, but ruthless in its exposition of the truth, which is always evolving and never what I think it is. This being is the Soul of Nature. It presents itself in many shapes, voices, and physical sensations on the psychic landscape. It can be male or female, or appear with a multitude of voices. It pulls images from the deepest recesses of my mind, and conjures unfathomable feelings and unthinkable states of being according to a most mysterious agenda of higher learning, or deeper becoming, or truer existence.

It introduces me to the gods, and I talk to them face to face, from god to god. It introduces me to myself, and I contemplate my infinite reflections, dying one by one. When everything is gone, I become a stainless universal mirror. And the Soul of Nature is another and the same mirror, in front of me, with nothing in between.

Magic mushrooms are not a drug. My dictionary defines a drug as "1. A substance used as a medicine in the treatment of disease. 2. A narcotic, especially one that is addictive" (*American Heritage*, p. 427). Magic mushrooms are neither.

Historically, magic mushrooms were used as aids in communicating with the supernatural. Sometimes the information coming from the inner levels reveals the source of diseases, and sometimes the inner guides prescribe treatments for them; but, they are not a medicine per se.

Magic mushrooms are not a narcotic. A narcotic is defined as a drug which dulls the senses, induces sleep, and becomes addictive with prolonged use. Magic mushrooms alert the senses, including those beyond the usual five; they eliminate fatigue and are absolutely non-addictive. They don't "fry your brain," but they do burn away your obsolete interpretations of life.

What then are the magic mushrooms? They are mind-enhancers and synchronizers; with their help man can pierce the veil of the social contracts that condition his perception of reality and see deeper into his own essence as well as into the forces and dynamics that shape life as we know it.

Why then are most people scared to death of them? Because when you eat them, they can scare you to death... This is no joke. A few have died from the fear produced by magic mushrooms, and a few others, like me, have been scared to death of their old selves.

Eating magic mushrooms means looking on in shock as your most basic assumptions about everything crumble. It means to experience the exacerbated bewilderment of one's reason to such an extent that it commits suicide by eating itself. It means going through the terror of the fall when the path you have been following confidently all your life disintegrates in the immensity, and I mean *immensity* of blackness.

It also means resurrecting the primeval consciousness in you—after everything else is gone. It is experiencing all the transitory glories of all the sacred texts in becoming your eternal self.

The magic mushrooms are not for everyone. Don Constantino told me that they help good people and afflict those with an evil heart. They can plunge people into their own hells. There is a protocol for their use and serious consequences for any negligence. You should not take them alone; ideally there should be a guardian whom you trust. You need to feel certain about what you want and advance with full caution. Dosage and rhythm, as well as understanding your astrological and personal cycles, is essential. Love, humility, and solid grounding constitute an indispensable platform for your journey, or you might not reassemble properly with all the new information gained from the experience. After your psychic voyage, you need time to integrate into your everyday life any new horizons the magic mushroom have opened up to you.

There are always some who rush into using the magic mushrooms with expectations of escaping, even for a few hours, the crushing pressures of material life. There is a deep hedonistic streak in their spiritual pursuits and that is not a good way to start. If you are looking to escape—whether that means achieving Christian salvation, Buddhist Nirvana, or the expectancy that the space brothers will come to rescue you—that means you dislike your life. And you always dislike your life when you can't change it. And if you can't change your life, it is because your power is not grounded. In this case, the mushrooms most likely are only going to amplify your lack of balance. "Space cadets" should avoid magic mushrooms unless determined to use them to find the cause of their split, and then work to put their brains together.

Average spiritual seekers have a variety of reasons for avoiding the magic mushrooms; most of these reasons will be based on misinformation, fear, or both.

Some think having mystical experiences with the help of the magic mushrooms are not the same as those without external aids. From my experience I can tell you that no mystical experience is the same as any other. There might be equivalencies, but they are always different. I have had equivalent mystical experiences with and without the magic mushrooms. The difference is that you can pull out from a self-induced ecstatic state easier; but, with the mushroom-induced experience the realizations are deeper. You are more fully present in the magical landscape.

Others say they do not want to depend on external aids. Their position is that you have to start always from scratch; everything should be earned out of your own sweat. They are afraid that if they depend on mushrooms today, they might not have access to them at some future time and would get stranded in the middle of nowhere. It is comparable to saying that they don't want to go to Paris because they might not have enough money next year to repeat the trip. These people do not realize how much they are addicted to food and water, electricity, and hundreds of other items for survival. Even their daily work and the money they earn is a condition for them to obtain that peace of mind essential to their spiritual practices.

In the end we are interdependent with everything else. Moreover, our real selves are all that surrounds us, and in the right frame of mind, we will always be able to bring to our lives what we need for our growth.

One of my teachers of magic once told me that drugs are there to show you the way and to take you there once, but then it is your responsibility to learn to walk on your own. I think this is excellent advice.

The basic truth about the avoidance of magic mushrooms in the pursuit of higher awareness is the irrational, organic fear of the lower self. It is terrified because it knows it is going to be disintegrated. The seemingly innocent Greek axiom, "Man, know thyself," is the most challenging and difficult of all the quests. Everyone wants to look up and talk to God, but most are afraid to look inside.

I address the basic fear of the magic-mushroom experience by describing the fear that comes from being trapped on a negative magic-mushroom journey. Yet on this transformational psychic voyage I found the devil and learned to live with him.

Upon awakening the morning of the experience, I saw a fleeting image of Dionysus, the Greek god of freedom and everlasting youth. I meditated for a full hour and accessed a high level which gave me lots of energy. All this made me think about controlling the magic-mushroom journey to bring the archetype of the Divine Child fully into my awareness. My purpose was to express the archetype of the Divine Child as much as possible in my life.

Before the ingestion of the mushroom I cleansed myself ceremonially with copal incense. This connected me to the Mesoamerican Indian memory of nature. I saw prehispanic universes filled with inconceivable beings, some of them beautiful, luminous, kaleidoscopic, others of a low-energy level. I saw myself going from mansion to mansion in an infinite treasure house of Aztec/Toltec/Zapotec/Mixtec images. After awhile I realized the futility of all that. The visions were nice, but there was nothing transcendental about them. I summoned all my will power, and with full intention tried to force the energy of the Divine Child to come into my body, twice. I was unsuccessful.

The quality of the visions changed after that display of will. I was plugged into the collective memory bank of deceased prehispanic warrior-priests who, in and after life, trained their wills to make their way in life, and into death, always as they wished. They had forced the world and nature to obey them. They liked my display of will and I was being accepted in their all-boys' club.

For a moment I felt proud of my accomplishment. I could not bring the Divine Child, but my efforts were recognized and admired... Soon my feelings warned me that something very serious and dangerous was about to take place. Somehow I felt that the energy of that place was negative. There was a terrible tension in keeping the will in focus against all the erosive forces of the universe, and a painful sense of loneliness. All that was an outcome of the egotistical will of those warriors.

I made my last supreme effort to change the vision into that of the Divine Eternal Child, but I only received memories of one of those warriors, or the one of them who got inside me. For a moment I assumed the image of a priest in a prehispanic ceremonial, wearing a mask made with the skin of a dead man. I was performing an inane ancient ritual representing the renewal of life. But the underlying cosmology of the ritual was all based on the futility of human existence, a grayish resignation to the cosmic cycles that overpower the feeble human condition—a kind of primitive existentialism of eternal depression and hopelessness.

I shook off the disgusting shell of the priest and decided to move for awhile to change the psychic frequency I was in. I came out of my improvised temple to talk with Luisa, but was careful not to tell her about all the negative energy I was contacting since I did not want to worry her. I lay down to rest for awhile close to her heart, but I could not. As soon as I put my head on her chest a most-horrid mantis-shaped being emerged from Luisa's heart, uncoiling its putrid essence, displaying ever-changing protrusions that moved like agonizing worms continuously bending at the weirdest angles. I clearly knew those protrusions represented unending cunning strategies to achieve ultimate control of everything around it. It grew out of Luisa's heart until it became the size of the whole room.

I knew instinctively this represented the ultimate tyrant. It was an evil thoughtform created by the interaction between Luisa and a very close relative who always tried to dominate her will; the thoughtform was attached to her because of her sensitivity and compassion. All her life she had to wrestle with this monster who incessantly tried to keep her under his vision and his way of life. Her extraordinary sense of purpose had kept her on the side of freedom, but the crafty attempts of manipulation threw her many times into emotional confusion and despair. This had created a wound in her heart, and the poison of criticism had nourished the evil creature nesting at the core of her etheric body.

As tactfully as I could, I described my vision to her. I was worried she would regard all my sharing as pure paranoia. But she acknowledged she had been feeling emotional and physical pain in the heart for many days, and that it was always aggravated whenever she longed to communicate in a real and deep way with this relative of hers.

The vision grew in malignancy and power. I became aware of the transpersonal energy feeding the visions. It was the great oppressor, the Devil himself. It was very curious that our ten-year-old child, precognitive and curious as no other, had asked me just the day before if I had at any time seen the devil in my meditations. I had never seen the devil before, and now he was in front of me, plunging me in depths of darkness without parallel in my whole emotional history. It was sheer terror.

I realized this overpowering entity was an archetype I had been fighting all my life, unconsciously. I had fashioned my life as a hero does his; all my manly traits were barriers against the monster. I had learned to keep him at a bay by slaying all the little dragons along my life. My courage, determination, focus, and boldness were just shields held up in perpetual battle against the multi-headed monster.

I discovered that through my efforts to keep him out of my life, I had become a little like him. I had fought his avid, incessant, overpowering thrust with a tendency to manipulate my life and my environment. I had developed the same obsession to be in control of my life. I had tightened my personality to such an extreme that the Divine Child would never surface in a psychological environment like mine. I recognized that I was very much like a tyrant sometimes, and at my best I restricted my own growth by forcing it always along lines of development I felt necessary for my dealings against the forces of chaos.

Fear was all around and inside me. I knew I could not keep the monster outside me anymore. Out of fear I had built my defenses, and although I had learned to become an oppressor myself, the root of all my behavior was plain, abstract, organic terror. Yes, I was a hero and an oppressor, but I was also a victim of my unconscious fears. I had learned to silence fears with the display of force to the point that I was not aware of my fears anymore. I had always been courageous, but only because I had buried my fears in layer upon layer of rigid strategies to deal with life. This armored approach to life was a burden I couldn't take any longer.

The first thing I did was to accept the fear. I cried like a baby in Luisa's lap. By honestly admitting I was afraid, afraid of everything, I could feel how this fear came from my mother's side, how I absorbed it when still in her womb as she crossed oceans of uncertainty and endured numerous environmental, economical, and emotional storms.

In synchrony with the experience, my mother called me long distance precisely at that same moment. I told her about my state and how I could feel her past confusion and fear during her pregnancy with me. She confirmed my psychic findings and assured me that the network of love I belonged to would keep me safe even in the midst of madness.

As I plunged myself in full consciousness into infinite holograms of terror, into the body of the devil himself, I started to realize that fear was a great master of linear time. It was everywhere.

Fear was behind us, perpetually driving all humanity to escape from it; civilization existed because human beings had been scared of winter, pain, disease, starvation, and so forth.

Fear was left and right, above and below as it shaped human personality in its battle against the environment. It trained humanity in the development of power and determination, so that we learned to choose and work for the conditions we wanted from life out of fear of those we did not.

Fear was also in front of us, helping us to recognize our human limits, telling us when to stop, when it was unsafe to go forward. Fear was at the root of our instinct for self-preservation.

I realized that fear existed as a primitive, abstract emotion, and that it also continues to incarnate in our physical lives. All tyranny is simply a manifestation of unaccepted, unrecognized fears. Tyrants are born of fear and prey on their victims' fears to preserve their own existence. If we recognize and deal with our fears within ourselves, they will not manifest on physical reality in the form of tyrants we have to fight. When people say they can't do something because the spouse, the job, or someone else is preventing them, the truth is they are afraid of going forward, but do not recognize this fact. So instead, unconsciously they bring into their lives an outside oppressor.

For those ready to finish their training in three-dimensional reality, fear also indicates the barriers to infinity. Once you have developed a sense of purpose, if fear is in your way, there you should go, but never with the blind courage of a hero, never obsessed to meet with challenge. Fear should be faced with the awe of one about to enter holy ground. Fear is an indicator you are about to break into a new area of consciousness. You can understand and even love fear as a signpost that stands at the end of your personal territory—it is the gate to the magical kingdom, and adventure awaits as you go through its doors. The Divine Child is on the other side.

As I was understanding all this, a deep sense of worthlessness came over me. I realized I had distrusted everything; I could not have faith in my new realizations, nor in the comforting voice of my wife, fear being also the root of mistrust, apprehension another mask of the same old fear. This time, guided by a hint from Luisa, I went to see what I was afraid of.

Obviously I was afraid of losing myself, my mind, my reason, my strength against chaos, my sense of purpose. I could become a victim. But going deeper into my fear I asked myself the question: What is this sense of "Me" I am defending so zealously? I have known for a long time that my sense of "Me" is just a construction of the mind, with no substance of its own. I realized I was stupidly defending an old, worn-out possession! "But if I relinquish the 'Me,' how do I keep from being lost in the infinite labyrinths of transpersonal consciousness?" I asked the invisible guides of my process. And the answer to this was shown to me.

I saw a new dimension being opened to me. From there I felt the consciousness of Don Juan, Carlos Castaneda's teacher, and others within his vanished group, supervising the process as if from another dimension. He then said, "He has taken all that he can. Let's heal the opening now."

At that point they showed me a vision of the archetype of the *nagual*, or the psychic self as the human guide in the maze of the beyond. The *nagual* can become everything; he can dive into any of those fantastic worlds and become a citizen forever. But he has a sense of purpose, a vision he shares with his crew.

I saw a magnificent representation of the *nagual's* party as a crew sailing toward the dream of freedom. But not the freedom I had understood before. For me freedom was a linear escape from oppressive circumstances, a continuous restlessness, because as soon as I had built a new reality, it became a prison of stagnation and decay. They showed me their vision of freedom as an ease of movement and being despite any circumstance, plus the ability to change circumstances at will to serve the purpose at hand.

The cosmic currents the boat sails along are composed of pure fear of the unknown. The party keeps together by the focus of their goal. The *nagual* explores the way and gives all a sense of purpose and direction. The feminine members of the group bring coherency and anchor the *nagual's* explorations since he is lost without feminine help. The *nagual* can become, or bring about, anything necessary for the development of the members of his group. He is a catalyzer, a joker in the cosmic card game of evolution in this sense; his own definition derives from his interrelationship with the group.

They showed me the function of the *nagual* as that of an orchestra director, organizing the focus of the group members' powers of mental creation so that they may together play the melody present since time immemorial. The melody is the flow of the river of the evolution of consciousness. The *nagual* is that archetypal, eternal character in this eternal melody.

I felt the power of the archetypal current of the *nagual* living in me and acting through me, bypassing my humanness, my egocentric views. I felt unworthy of this honor; I felt the weight of the responsibility to become a suitable vessel for such a magnificent and sublime power. I understood that the best way to act in this situation was to get myself out of the way, letting the archetype act through me on its own. I accepted it.

It became clear to me how I was already the captain of the ship that Carlos mentioned eleven years ago. STAR*LIFE is that ship; I sail with my indispensable crew—even the cleaning lady is an essential part of the whole. I would be nothing without them.

After all these realizations I felt a powerful upsurge of this energy emanating from all around my energy field. Later it anchored in my heart. The sensation was of an unwavering flow fostering growth and evolution in all living beings, which could also be described as unconditional love. It was beautiful and painful at the same time, like the flaming heart of Jesus oppressed by the crown of thorns.

Although I could identify myself with this basic "guru" force, I realized at once that the main mistake of many saviors of humanity was to identify themselves exclusively with this frequency, to accept being sacrificed in the blissful bitterness of a paternal love. Some of this is necessary to bring cohesive force to life, to those around, but the guru stage can also be a prison for the expanding consciousness of a true seeker. It is just one of the many manifestations of the universal life that must flow from a true *nagual*. I learned that a higher, more real me is always changing, yet always the same.

This was the end of my mushroom experience. But I do not want to write about my experience with the devil without mentioning my experience with Jesus since I have seen the Master Jesus many times in my meditations and prayers. He always brings love, harmony, and balance. But the following experience happened out of the blue, and proved to be a real contact by virtue of its effect on my life. It happened when I was preparing to become a full-time metaphysics teacher. I was working in Florida under contract as a graphic designer, spending seven hours every day in front of a graphics computer. At lunchtime I always went to meditate in a small forest a hundred yards away from the building owned by GTE, my temporary employer.

For several days I had been feeling tired, breathless, and spacey. I had always been a healthy person, and it was very bothersome to feel unable to concentrate on my work. I clearly sensed that it was my body's way of letting me know I was out of alignment with my true will. Even so, I needed to survive my contract before I could make such a change, so I went to the forest that day and asked for help to keep myself going.

In my inner sight Jesus Christ appeared in all his glory for a second. He spoke the following words of wisdom: "Eat sardines," and then disappeared. I was still a strict vegetarian and didn't like the message, but you don't disobey the Master Jesus. So that afternoon I bought a can of the smelly fish I had always hated, and the next day I was fine. I included it in my diet for the rest of my stay in Florida and never experienced the symptoms again. Probably the Master Jesus knew I needed the B-complex, or iron, or calcium, or some other substance present in sardines. In any case, somebody the rank of Jesus Christ was needed to persuade such an obstinate vegetarian to change his eating habits!

10

OUTER DARKNESS AND THE MOVING CENTER OF LIGHT

When what you really are takes over you, it does so in unpredictable displays of its all-inclusive nature. You see the diverse facets of your original Self appearing in the glitter of nature, of surroundings, of relationships.

Often an aspect you haven't experienced before emerges, and the mind—the great juggler—rearranges your perceptions to include the new. This is the way revelations are blended into the cocktail of life; what could have been insight, inspiration, genius, drowns in the diffuse waters of today.

Sometimes what you really are reveals to you a mass of deep unveilings that seem alien to reason. Saturation in the beyond often dismembers the structure of your values, blunts the weapon of your judgment, and stirs the ancient swamp of your feelings. Feelings fly in all directions like aquatic birds at the end of the world. Look at those birds carefully. All of them are white; all of them are sacred ibises; all of them return to a peaceful land when the commotion is over.

This is the best time to feel you are alive, that you are more, that you are also all that your emerging memories bring. Don't waste these opportunities! Rejoice in your trepidation in the face of change! You *are,* not because you think, but because you feel, because you remember.

So, the next time the corrosive pressure of the Real You quickens your blood and unbalances your routines, don't cry "Chaos! Madness!" Instead, consider this misfortune a miracle. You are evolving! You, like the birds in the swamp, are displaying vitality and beauty, even in the fear of your flight.

Everybody needs to different degrees, predictability and innovation. Dissatisfaction arises when you are not able to control how much of each you want to experience growth in balance. When you give yourself to mass consciousness, it is like standing in line waiting to be served your daily portion of predictability and innovation: you never get exactly what you expect. You might then go and sit at the long table to complain to the others about the unfairness of the server, but you eat your portion anyway.

Religions, sects, bloodlines, and the state will always make you think you still live inside a feudal land, a nice, predictable environment where you only need to follow the rules of civilization to be free from the barbarians out there who rob and rape and kill. You just please the feudal lord, whether God or the taxation system, and he rewards you with peace. The light is inside with us; outside is the dark. Anything can happen. Booooo!

This scenario, however, is a lie. If your goal is to find complacency in routine entanglements, it might work for awhile, but the enclosed neo-feudal environment has never really been predictable; it merely gives the illusion of being so. Look at the news, then realize they are only feeding you the non-essentials: abuses and crimes are happening all the time from both the lawful and unlawful sides. There are barbarians both inside and outside the feudal land. Economies are more unstable than ever. You may get your portion of innovation when you least expect it, and then you will call it "chaos."

Yes, you can keep playing by the rules and build stronger defenses against the forces that undermine the security of your life: more money in the bank, a better alarm system, an even more-suspicious attitude that sees chaos threatening everything. However, these higher walls that protect you also limit and prevent your being able to escape them. In your striving to be more secure, you forget how to be.

It took me a long time to discard the cultural fears of my group-mind. When I was three-years old I told my mother I was going to be a magician. When I was five, upon winning first place at my first year at school, my father bought me a book on stage magic. I studied it for months! I always had the vague feeling there was something behind the illusions, as if they were the key to something holier, unfathomable. I never needed anybody to tell me that real magic was indeed a noble tradition, a path to deal with the illusions of matter as we know it. Unsupported, this interest was buried with a thousand others in my childhood.

By the time I was seven, I was trapped in the web of my group-mind. As customary in México, all children in school piously bought a vegetarian sandwich every Lenten Friday. It was not a religious school, but everybody believed that eating meat on those Fridays would put you in a state of "mortal sin." I thought it was stupid, and one day defied the whole school by boldly buying a bologna sandwich.

I could barely sleep for the next seven days! I had nightmares and spent many hours every night expecting some catastrophe to happen. The next Friday I religiously got a vegetarian sandwich and felt God was happy with me again. Even at that age I wondered why God should be so concerned with such an insignificant thing. And why the punishment only came out of my own guilt and fear.

Over the next years I always played by the rules. I was most of the time the best in the classroom, both in learning as well as conduct. I became a model of perfection and everybody admired my responsibility, correctness, and application. I assimilated the values of my world at a very early age, but often I was intuitive enough to notice how my behavior came from my need for admiration.

I learned that my drive to obtain first-place diplomas was based on the spirit of competition. I cared a lot for the reward, the quasi-orgasmic sensation at the podium when everybody was clapping their hands, telling me I was the best! Then I could see all the other children as defeated. I was the victorious warrior, ready for a pat on the shoulder from my tyrant-kings. I was able to question my approach to winning, but my insights did not change my behavior. I, knowingly, became a pleaser, and in the spirit of competition I became a "classroom climber."

I was externally submissive, but inside I longed for adventure and challenges of a higher nature. Over time earning first-place diplomas was not enough anymore. I was used to being the best, but now I wanted to be the best of the best. Also, to keep earning praise and admiration, my quest had to involve something different!

My determination to become a yogi and obtain *samadhi* came at age sixteen. I read a book that described *samadhi* as the highest goal a human being could achieve. It seemed good enough for me! I fashioned myself as becoming a supreme adept of the mysterious arts of yoga, amazing people all around. I didn't mind working diligently if I was going to receive admiration from others.

Soon I learned that becoming a yogi was not fashionable at all. My ascetic life prevented me from fitting in anywhere. No parties, no drinks, no spare time. Isolation was not easy to endure, but at the same time I was fascinated by the deeper aspects of mysticism; my petty interests converged with a true fascination with enlightenment. I was not going to stop, no matter what; yoga became a true path for me.

In those days the Universidad Autonoma de México had a very curious intellectual reputation; it was called the *apertura*, or the "opening." The school was supposed to emphasize an open-minded approach with as many as four areas in which to specialize: basic Marxism, Leninism, Maoism, and Castrism (nothing to do with castration). Long discussions were held in the classrooms as well as the corridors. To participate in the debates you had to fit into at least one of these categories. Teachers and fellow-students tried to indoctrinate me as soon as I arrived, but I always felt disgusted by the idea of equality. I was never clear about my political tendencies, but looking back I would have to define myself as an adherent of monarchy—provided I was the monarch!

Together with my political indefinition and my bizarre interests in yoga, I could find few people to talk to. It even cost me my high grades at school since the teachers did not like the "lack of philosophical foundation" in my creative work. But I could not do better. I had been born in a frontier city, a place where the values of both Mexican and American cultures were juxtaposed. It was a city continuously transforming. I had also been born into a time of change. So the best way I found to cope was to define myself as an undefined, free, and open individual.

This indefinition was good for my mind; it enabled me to consider multiple perspectives with cold detachment. My emotional life, however, suffered from a lack of belonging. There were no real models for me to follow. The gurus were in India, and anyway I never fully identified myself with the yogic way of life. Yoga was for me a series of techniques to achieve enlightenment, not an end in itself.

For some time I longed to become something I did not know how to define. Slowly, in the course of my studies and meditations, I recovered the image of the magician from the attic of my mind. Or it came over me, I should say. The world of the magus started to glow with renewed light, attracting my attention, luring me into worlds of reverie and fantasy. I read the books of the nineteenth-century French magicians who fascinated me. Their world felt so familiar! The model they presented was just what I was trying to define for myself, but the books did not present definite workable sequences.

I was lost in the middle of an immense puzzle of symbols and mystery, without a guide, without a map. I suffered attacks of both wonder and desperation. Studying those books I felt like a deceased Arab warrior in the Moslem paradise with eleven thousand virgins, not knowing where to start! I experimented with the construction of magical mirrors, my aim being to obtain guidance from the higher planes. I followed the procedures the best I could, but I never saw anything in them. Although I attributed the failure to my inexperience, I never blamed magic for this.

Those days I was a student of graphic design, as well as a teacher of yoga and astrology in México City. One night I dreamed I was in a holy place, watching one of my teachers of astrology. He was kneeling in front of some magical instruments, drawing triangles and other figures in the air, invoking my name three times, addressing me as a Master. I felt great energy coming into his magical circle, as if a wondrous but invisible being were landing in my teacher's magical circle. When my teacher felt satisfied with the results of his invocation, he focused his eyes on mine, and asked me in a very grave voice: "Is there something you want to know?"

My first reaction in the dream was to think he was fooling me, but soon I realized that this was a conscious dream and that all these images were symbols to help me understand that now was the precise moment to contact my future, more-evolved self.

I asked, "I want to know who have I been in previous lives. I want to know everything."

I expected to see flashbacks of different lifetimes, but instead I heard a most-powerful voice reverberating in the air. It said: "You come from the Bible from Moses. You have been here many times. Your path is the path of daring. ESTAR is an eleventh term according to A."

I woke up and dutifully registered my dream.

I felt the word ESTAR was like a magical name for me. I recognized this last sentence had a hidden Kabalistic meaning. The only thing I knew about Kabalah in those days was that it was the embodiment, in complex numerological formulas, of the secret traditions of Israel. Needless to say, I set myself to investigate those Kabalistic traditions after this dream.

Four years later when I was living in Tijuana, I unlocked the meaning of this esoteric sentence I had dreamed. I had recently discovered Aleister Crowley's books, one of which was about Kabalah and contained numerological equivalents of the letters. I used this table to find the numeric value of the mysterious word "ESTAR" which in Spanish means "to be placed at." I was astounded when the addition of its letters amounted to 666.

By this time I knew 666 was one of Crowley's preferred numbers. Eleven was also a cherished number, the number of energy in the process of change, and this number also appeared in my dream. "A" could refer to "Aleister," or to "Aiwass," the name of his Guardian Angel; or to the "Astrum Argentum," the name for an invisible, atemporal order he said he represented on earth.

Not only that, using another numerological sequence based on the Major Arcana of the Tarot Cards, "ESTAR" rendered 93, a number meaning "love" on three levels, another number Crowley used to define his influence on the world.

By anagrammatizing the word ESTAR I found two other striking parallels with Crowley's magical universe. All this was too much to be coincidence, I thought. It was a clear indication that the contact with my higher self in that conscious dream four years before brought veiled information about an invisible, transpersonal magical school unknown to me in those days.

The same contact with my higher self had told me my path was that of daring. I thought I was daring enough with my extravagant disciplines of vegetarianism and yoga, but now the message was clear to me, I should dare to plunge myself deeper into the magical universe of the Beast 666, as Crowley used to call himself.

I pondered on this for days. My emotions were all over my skin. But I might not have acted on any of this if there had not been another revelation and synchrony that set me onto that path. My boldness at that time was only enough to perform a ritual in my bedroom, using one of Crowley's books as a link. In that ritual I challenged the invisible guides of the magical school to which he belonged to send me a real, incarnate teacher.

As far back as I can remember I used to scribble the word "ANTES" (meaning "before" in Spanish). It always came automatically when testing the sharpness of pencils, or when I was waiting for the ink to flow from pens, or without thinking, over dusty windshields. Soon after my magical invocation during one of my conscious dreams, I saw this word in big red letters all over a black horizon; then the letters rearranged themselves into the word "SETAN."

"SETAN" was the correct word, since "SET" is the name of the prince of darkness in Egyptian mythology. "Yes, I heard the message!" I said ironically to the invisible guides—seeing Hell opening before me, and knowing that I had to dare to go in.

Two weeks after this dream a psychic friend who lived in a beautiful city one hour from Tijuana called me. "My brother," she said, full of excitement, "I have just met the man who is going to be your teacher."

My friend did not know anything about Crowley or my ritual, but she was correct. I went to see the man she recommended so highly, and I felt an instantaneous affinity with him. He pulled out Crowley's Tarot card pack at the exact time I was asking him if he knew anything about Crowley. He spread the cards in the Celtic pattern, and the card that came out as the one representing the long-term results of my spiritual life was that of the Magus. The man was indeed a link to the Astrum Argentum atemporal school of magic and gave me all the information I needed to begin my practical work.

Crowley was the first one to bring to the civilized world a philosophy of life that integrated both the light and dark aspects of humanness. Most spiritual traditions still regard the sordid aspects of life and being human as antagonistic to the pure, high, divine dimensions. Matter is defined as impure, sorrowful, or illusionary. Entering on the spiritual path is considered even now a matter of choosing good and rejecting evil. Whole cosmogonies have been created from this dualistic perception. Spiritual patriarchs of all times have always warned against the dark deceptive powers that lure us into entrapment and bondage, declaring that the only way to be safe is to follow the disciplines and regulations of spiritual ideologies created for tribal survival—not for the development of all the possibilities of humanness. Crowley was the first one in modern times to point out the sacredness of the personal drives, and introduced a way to coordinate them into power to achieve spiritual, individual aims.

Most spiritual paths pit society against nature—society aligned with the future, the human order, sanctioned by God; Nature is regarded as the past, the spontaneous, primitive, illogical world of the devil. Crowley's cosmology included demons, too, but these were of a different order. Every factor of life that distracts from the course of the integrated, spiritualized will is regarded as a vampire, an individualized tentacle of the universal demon of dispersion. The vampires lurk in the glitter of society. The true will is the Titan chained to the bowels of the earth, producing from time to time earthquakes that shake the personality in the form of instincts. Our task is to free the Titan, to align the forces of the personality to the will of the immortal being, and live a purposeful life in the pursuit of the fulfillment of our intrinsic, peculiar natures. Crowley's magical universe is coherent if you take the time to learn the symbolic language of the diverse spiritual traditions of the West.

Regarding my own interpretation of these spiritual stages of growth, I see the individual first standing at the center of his/her narrow understanding of existence, surrounded by the hows and whys of past generations, the indoctrination received since birth. This individual thinks s/he is in harmony with life, in righteousness with God because s/he is in relative stability within society. For man indeed has made God in his/her own likeness, and every heaven has been depicted as the most-desirable place for those who follow the most cherished values of society.

The higher forces of evolution increase the life power that springs from your own inner nature; this can make you feel as if you are the caught bird in the golden cage or the snake in its old skin. At your side is another serpent, Lucifer, the Light-bearer; he promises that you can become like a god if you dare to disobey the god of your environment and taste the fruit of questioning. Is it good or is it bad? Once you question, the process can't be reversed, and inevitably you will feel strangled by the established framework; you will need to leave your old skin behind or die. You are becoming a serpent yourself, accursed as all of its kind. You will be cast out.

On your way to exile, you will probably visit many temporary shelters: another marriage, idiosyncratic clubs, support groups, exotic schools of thought, New Age circles... At times you may think you have found your truth, but the curse does not leave you. You keep growing so that your skin can't contain you anymore; you need to renew your skin again and again. Change is the rule of your life.

After some time you look more and more like a serpent. Now your eyes are open all the time. You are becoming wiser, and inevitably keep going farther and farther, deeper and deeper into the outer darkness.

When the darkness is so intense you cannot see anymore, not even your own body, your eyes of wisdom lose their power. In the outer abyss there are no landmarks, and only one thing is certain: You have become your own shadow.

Being in the darkness helps you lose the boundaries of form; you feel you encompass the darkness. Your skin doesn't strangle you anymore. In the darkness you don't need to look attractive; you forget about continuous renewal. You learn to be, just to be. From this beingness, immortal light emerges truly from the center of your self, from your heart, your own light, the light of your being. At this stage you no longer care about how you look, but if somebody where to observe you now, he would see a cosmic snake biting its own tail—an entirely self-contained universe. The promise of the serpent of paradise is now fulfilled. You are the god of your own universe, and your inner light feeds the worlds.

One of the basic aberrations of our culture is that the only strategies for life are considered to be either a permanent yielding to the Lord of Light or a fierce battle against the Forces of Darkness. In this context the word of the Lord is all the collective assumptions that stabilize our society; the Lord Himself manifests in authority figures such as your parents or your boss. Darkness is everything that threatens established order.

According to this view, you can specialize in yielding or in fighting; you may choose between the path of the saint or the hero. In practice, however, both paths result in dead ends.

The saint is often the martyr. Today you can find parallels in this pattern in all those nice, kind, spiritual people who yield too much, of whom everybody takes advantage.

The hero is always killed by the forces of chaos, as in the permanent cyclical change of day and night, spring and winter; the hero will prosper for a time, but being part of a larger process, he doesn't have a chance at permanent achievement. There are many real proofs of this pattern in the lives of high-level executives, who, even though they succeed in some/many ways, are always defeated by death.

These two strategies are seen in the mundane as well as in the spiritual dimensions of humanity. There is no lasting fulfillment in either. The main problem is that everyone either yields to or fights for an external, false light.

In the long run it is never wise to obliterate the ego in favor of the light of established social contracts, nor determine to kill all the emotional or physiological dark dragons that bring social chaos. The real challenge today is to acknowledge the many facets of your humanness until you find the underlying current that gives meaning to your life, then follow it, dancing with your fears, thriving on the adventure of the path of darkness into the real light of being.

In the outer darkness, logic and social values no longer help you find your course. Similar to sailing without points of reference, it's really scary. The only way to the inner light comes from inside, from intuition as manifested through purified feelings, feelings not tainted by old beliefs.

The following anecdote gives a revealing look at just such an experience I had in the inner worlds of meaning with the help of the magic mushrooms.

Before taking the elixir I was trembling with panic, fear assaulting me from every corner of my mind. I was much better prepared to recognize and deal with my fear this time, although it took a supreme effort of will to take the magic potion. When I put it to my lips, I heard the voice of the Goddess telling me that everything would be fine because she would supervise the whole process. Since her soft voice soothed me a little, I then performed the definitive act that put me past the point of no-return, and indeed, no one ever returns the same from a magic-mushroom journey. Soon, a dweller of the magical dimensions whom I identified as the *nagual* Julian (the teacher of the teacher of Carlos Castaneda), told me that behind the wall of fear was a level of feeling I had been repressing all my life. Now was the time to learn to trust my feelings, to live by them, to understand that anything in life may be perceived as a paradox when the mind runs with enough energy to reach thesis and antithesis simultaneously.

Entering the dimensions of timelessness, the visions start. I am getting closer and closer to a zone of confusing and painful feelings about life and death. Life and death here form a single emotional field where both feel limiting—once you are born, you are *forced* to live and you are *forced* to die. Related to this is also the fear of the unexpected possibilities of life and death.

The force field of the Mother Archetype dominates the whole field of sensations, but it is a bloody mother. Images of prehispanic women in labor flash into my awareness, together with closeups of newborns covered with blood and bodily excretions. Everything is hopeless and full of despair. The inevitability of the dullness of life and/or the darkness of death permeates the gloomy atmosphere of the place.

I intuitively recognize that this frequency of feeling is a door to something. I know I have to go through it, but I am fearful to the bone. I do not want to abandon myself to this painful bundle of sensations. The voice of the Goddess comes again, this time much clearer than before the mushroom potion created its effect on me: "You have come to me countless times since the beginning of existence. You have crossed this gate many times in your spiritual journeys along many incarnations. You are one of my sons, the quintessential shaman; your cosmic role is predetermined and you are an inhabitant of these worlds as you are of the world of matter. Come to me; surrender to me; I enfold you and protect you."

LUIS DE LA LAMA

free will?

In no time I go through a vision of the sorrows of life and death ... I emerge as the shamanic soul walking in the other world. Father Spirit and Mother Earth recognize my eternal self giving me a shield and bow and arrows for the journey to come. I now know my mission on twentieth-century earth. I become aware of my function in the universe: I am a guide and a healer of souls.

Then the visions change. On my last inner journey accepting my fear opened up my nature's dark side. This time I am able to reconcile it to my everyday self to achieve a broader perspective of myself. This new perspective is paradoxical; it includes the abyss and the light. I see how all my actions are the result of an almost infinite set of variables of archetypal, biological, sociological, and psychological origin, how free will as commonly understood is a platitude, a naive idea to help us maintain the idea of the individual self in a universe where we are agents of vast forces beyond our comprehension, forces that shape our destiny.

I learn that in the universe everything is in an indivisible state of Oneness by virtue of the principle of cosmic interdependence. Free will as an explanation for the source of our actions is as primitive and as false as the belief that babies come into the world brought by the stork or that they grow out of cabbage patches.

But there are ways to avoid the sense of hopelessness resulting from the recognition that free will is a lie. Instead of becoming paralyzed at the sight of these colossal, macrocosmic powers, our individualized consciousness can learn to play a game, the game of gliding along these immense lines of force. However, the chief rule of this game is right perception.

Logic cannot help us on this higher energy level. As evolution of spiritual awareness unfolds, the rational mind becomes dysfunctional and cannot make decisions due to the imponderable factors that only the purified feelings can recognize. Nonetheless, such feelings should not be distorted by aberrations stemming from an interpretation of phenomena or situations caused by old emotional scars. Therefore, evolution of consciousness requires a cleansing of the interpretive faculties of the mind to allow intuitive expression through feelings that convey a clear sense of direction for action, or inaction, if that's the case.

For the rest of the night I was able to see paradox in everything. I realized that each individual phenomenon of the universe can be interpreted in a multitude of ways, if you are lucid and honest enough. The rational mind can never find the ultimate interpretation of anything because there will always be many meanings—all equally valid from different levels of perception.

Yet becoming aware of life's multiple meanings at this state of higher awareness often paralyzes our capacity for action! The only way to get out of this paralyzed state is to recognize the relativity of all interpretations and to trust the positive feelings that occur when discovering the correct direction for action.

At this stage, we are forced to recognize our inability to synthesize rationally these multiple vectors of the world of consciousness. From this point on it is only possible to rely on the unifying power of intuition to bring us into the sphere of feeling.

From this higher level of awareness I am simultaneously aware of all the petty personality traits that might be the source of our personal decisions, as well as our higher, more-noble ideals, and the archetypal, biological, and social currents that affect our actions.

For example, I can see how writing this book comes out of diverse psychological processes, and, therefore, simultaneously entertains a variety of potential meanings that color my work, i.e., my petty search for fame and fortune, as well as the need to structure my new views of existence and the processes of my life, etc. My writing, in this case, is a trap I use to catch the fleeting perceptions of the higher worlds in conscious meaning, a trap I set for myself, a conceptual enclosure that may prevent further expansion. Like Narcissus, I can be frozen in the reflection of my present understanding and incapacitate myself in transcending the views presented in this book.

My act of writing is at the same time a song to universal life, an echo of the Eternal Original sound as it bounces back from the microcosmic consciousness of one of its creations.

My writing is simultaneously the desperate efforts of a feeble human mind trying to establish and assert itself, the act of making sense and establishing understanding in a universe of wonders, and the magnificent act of God when it looks at itself through human eyes. And, of course, it is also the noble effort of a compassionate nature trying to share his findings with other fellow travelers in the perpetually nebulous realm of meaning.

This revelation of the coexistence of meanings and values renders all my judgments ineffective. There are no definitive truths. Why bother looking for any? A great weight is lifted from me, as if all my sclerotic thoughts explode at once and the veins of awareness burst in the anti-gravity field of chaos. I know the primitive instrument called logic has no use in this domain. Instinctively the answer comes: Trust in your feelings; this is the only answer.

Yes. The feelings! ... the feelings! ... but I have no experience with them. My mind is always running after achievements of one kind or another. My mind is always building structures of meaning. My mind is always thinking in me. Everything I think is always in relation to me! I recognize my experience with feelings is very poor. I learned at a very early age to deal with things once I had succeeded in packing them in conceptual boxes, according to their function.

Thus, if I am in a forest, I ignore all stimuli, except those relevant to keep me on course. If I am forced to deal with a tree because it is in my way, I perceive the tree only as an obstacle. If I am hot, I perceive it as potential shade. If I am cold, I perceive it as potential firewood. But I am unable to open myself and perceive how I feel about the tree. The same with people; the same with everything. The basis for screening out my feelings is fear of the painful ones.

I interpret things, people, events, and situations as sets of functions, and judge them accordingly. If I open myself to perception through feeling I can be easily hurt; so, before dealing with anything in life, first I must cast my net of egotistical supremacy over it, then I pack it in the box of my reason, and finally I label my catch according to its function in my life. Isn't that miserable trickery?

Somehow I become aware that this Machiavellian strategy to avoid pain and achieve order in my life is anchored in the structure of language itself. Names and adjectives allow me to surround and cage the dangerous bundles of sensations that constitute the phenomena I encounter in my daily life. I have a vision in which I see the words as stepping stones on my journey through life, but the stones themselves are floating in an immense dark abyss of mystery and madness.

I hear the voice of the divine entities that supervise my spiritual growth: "Are you ready to leave the safety of language?" The sight of that abyss puts me in total confusion; I do not know what to say. I sweat profusely; an organic terror paralyzes my answer.

The voice of the Goddess comes to me again: "Why do you fear a level of communication the deepest part of you has always shared with animals, plants, and other invisible living creatures?" I let myself be conducted by the Goddess as a child who has hurt himself, is in shock and fear, yet remains obediently with his Mother while she tends the wound. She takes me to an area of consciousness that is soft and warm, pure and nurturing.

Yes. The feelings! . . . How can I feel? . . . How can I learn to feel? . . . I look all around for help. I am now experiencing the grace of the Goddess, but am hopelessly unable to incorporate Her presence into my being. I feel the agonizing isolation of being a man, the abysmal difference between the sexes. I pray to the Goddess for help, desperately seeking a way out of the male thought processes.

After awhile I open my eyes, and there she is! Materialized in front of me, the magnificent Aphrodite embodied in Luisa, who is lying naked on the couch, languorously playing with a cat. Aphrodite is often depicted as a breathtakingly beautiful naked woman escorted by leopards or other felines. The sight of my Twin-Soul at this moment is in marvelous synchrony; it is for me mind-blowing proof of the omnipresence of the body of the Goddess.

I realize how my wife is my teacher in the arts of feeling. I go to her and humbly confess the shallowness, the flatness of my feelings. I tell her I recognize how vain I have been in playing guru with her when she has much more to teach me. I remember our beautiful house as an extension of the exquisite qualities of her personality. My life is dry and unattractive; my aura is robotic compared to hers! I feel smaller and smaller in front of the archetypal woman . . . until I become nothing.

Unexpectedly, for a brief moment, I experience feminine consciousness from the inside. I feel as a woman feels! (or so I believe up to this day). It is just for a fraction of a second, but it is enough. I emerge as the divine androgyne; I see myself as a reconciliation of all opposites. My consciousness can contain all paradoxes without conflict! I become the alchemical Mercury, the winged god of the Hermeticists. For a brief moment I see Thoth, the Egyptian god of wisdom, supervising the development of my drastic changes in awareness.

I am free! My sensation of freedom expands to infinity, and my consciousness with it . . . Suddenly, I reach the Center. My Real Self radiates from every cell in my body . . . I am also in every atom. I am dynamic peace, eternal outpouring. I am as Knum, the divine potter . . . Osiris, the God of life and death. I have been sacrificed and now am experiencing a resurrection beyond the realm of duality.

I incarnate the center of creation. The source of life pours its divine essence through my very existence. I become the Tree of Life, the immutable maker of worlds. I realize I have been acting in this mode since the beginning of time. Realizing the universality of my self clears away my anxiety about the future. I have always been there, behind the scenes of manifestation, providing life to all that exists. Why have I been so deluded as to worry about earning a living?

Laughing at my recognition of the paradox of being in a state of divine consciousness (that is at the same a universal truth and the best of the egocentric trips, a monument to megalomania), I go to bed.

I am unable to sleep, so I take advantage of my higher state to explore communication with other beings who have realized their wholeness . . . I learn from them that the next task is to become a conscious creator of a new universe. For this you should choose one or two basic qualities you want your universe to possess, to identify with those qualities to the point of becoming the source of them. You embody those qualities by merging with the feelings associated with them.

I glimpsed the individual universes of several of my teachers. For example, I became aware how the *nagual* Julian set himself to become the Cosmic Joker, the absolutely spontaneous laughter of creation. The *nagual* Carlos Castaneda is a softer, diaphanous emanation of freedom. I realize how he gave me the gift of freedom by the same act I first thought would lead me to darkness. By not taking me into his tortuous world of procedures to achieve freedom, he let me be free at once, free to explore and achieve on my own. What a sublime and magnificent gift! I honored him in brotherhood and gratitude.

Together with my wife, I am building a universe of love and abundance. I am learning to become the universal provider, the tree of the fulfillment of all wishes. Carlos is building a universe of freedom by detachment; I want to build a universe of freedom by absolute satisfaction. My guru today is the cat. I feel he might be closer to the center of creation than I am. He is himself by doing nothing! He sustains his universe (where I am included) by his mere existence. He is indeed a powerful being!

☙❧☙❧☙❧☙❧☙❧

EPILOGUE

My inner fire is in harmony now. It burns like the warmth of life that I experience everyday. My life is very busy because I never run out of ideas, although the rush, the anxiety, is gone. Instead, I have a serene exhilaration. I know what peace is. I have learned about faith in the wisdom of Nature and this has emptied a good part of my mind. Now I can lose myself in the activities I enjoy. Thanks to a miraculous reorganization of my inner drives—brought about by my past spiritual disciplines and the deep workings of the magic mushrooms—what I enjoy doing now is also beneficial for others, so I am seldom confronted by difficult choices in my actions.

I still enjoy ceremonial magic in all its forms. When in our seven-day intensive workshops, the students, all in white robes, meet each morning and we invoke the archangels of the metaphysical elements. We all know we are doing real magic. I like to think then that I am demonstrating the basics of an ancient art that one day should flourish in each one as an individual, original way to transcendence. When I feel my universal self alive in the souls of all the participants, I know who I am. When I teach them how to wield the invisible forces of life, I feel heaven and earth in harmony.

I also enjoy exploring new ways to bring about the development of awareness and the positive qualities of existence that come with it. Luisa and I are designing new workshops, and I feel several other books pushing their way into manifestation from the abstract regions of my mind. We have much to do, and most of it is fun.

In my meditations when I breathe in I know how it feels to be the Absolute One; when I breathe out I know how it feels to be All in Everything. Sometimes I surprise God when he looks at his creation through my eyes. Whenever I pay attention to this miracle, however, God goes away, and this is also okay. I accept myself as I am now.

At work, I am in love with Life; at rest, I am One with It.

INDEX

A

A Dictionary of Angels 70. *See also* Davidson, Gustav
A—— 42, 49, 175
Adam 60
Æther 56, 59, 60, 62, 64, 90, 92, 99, 115
Agni 81, 82, 104
Agni Yoga Museum 81
Amoun 101
Angelic magic 55, 56, 65
Angels 5, 15, 51, 56, 62, 68-71, 78-80, 90, 92, 99, 104, 108, 112, 115, 143, 151-152, 154, 175
Anubis 71-72, 74, 96, 98, 105
Aphrodite 99, 186. *See also* Venus
Archangels 90, 189
Archetypal energies 116, 117
Archetypes 38, 100, 141, 160, 162, 165, 166, 181
Artemis 89
Ashram 82, 134
Astrology 6, 37, 45, 55, 67, 75, 87, 149, 174
Auras 4, 7, 51, 68, 70, 75, 106, 113, 116, 118, 123-124, 127, 131, 133-134, 136, 139, 150. *See also* Energy Fields
Avatar of Synthesis 51
Aztec 160

B

Babalon 100
Bagawan Rajneesh 134
Bailey, Alice 152
Baja California 79
Baphomet 74
Beings of Light 56, 79, 80
Biomagnetic healing 99
Blavatsky, Helena Petrova 78

C

Cannabis 44, 155
Castaneda, Carlos 11, 33-37, 46-48, 71, 80, 165-166, 181, 187-188
Chakras 51, 80, 116, 122, 123, 124, 126, 127, 128, 130, 135, 138, 144
Christ consciousness 141
Christian Rosencreutz 100
Christina 90, 91
Clairvoyance 75, 129, 156
Cosmic Activations 5, 96, 115, 116, 117, 118
Cosmic consciousness 34, 50, 72, 184
Count St. Germain 97. *See Also* Prince Rakozi

191

Cronus 59
Crowley, Aleister 88, 175-177

D

Dakini 100
Deneb 117
Derrumbes 19
Dignities 115
Dionysus 160
Divine Child 15, 160-163, 165
Don Constantino 12-13, 15-18, 158
Don Juan 11, 34-35, 37, 46, 165

E

Eagle 36, 38-43, 46-52, 54, 59, 80-81, 89, 96
Elements 92, 115-116
Energy fields 4, 17, 34, 80, 99, 121-122, 124, 127, 136, 166. *See also* Auras
Ensenada 152-153
Etheric vampire 134
Evil King 16
Existentialism 161
Extraterrestrials 122, 134, 142

F

Five Phases of Energy 115
Florida 92, 167, 168
Free will 182

G

Gematria 70, 91
Goddess 49, 85, 86, 87, 88, 89, 90, 92, 94, 95, 99, 102, 103, 104, 115, 180, 181, 186
Golden Book of St. Germain 97
Gray Wolf 136-139

Great Abyss 49
Great Guru 149-150
Green fairy 86
Guardian Angel 68, 70, 151-152, 154, 175
Gustav Davidson 71

H

Hashish 154-155
Hatha yoga 67, 149-150
Hawk 38, 44, 62
Healing procedures 17
Hedonism 100
Hero 52, 72, 88, 162-164, 179-180
High Magic 98
Higher Self 91, 102, 111, 138, 176
Hitler 151
Hitler's son 151-154
Holy Death 77
Holy Grail 151-152
Holy Spear 151-152
Horus 38, 41, 50, 94
Human Energy Systems 122. *See also* Schwarz, Jack

I

I Ching 53-54, 95
Illuminism 100
Isis 4, 49, 61, 89, 94-96, 102

J

Jesus Christ 3-4, 15, 148, 168
Julian 181, 187
Jung 68

K

Kabalah 75, 89, 113, 175

Kabalistic (magic and numerology) 68, 70, 80, 90, 91, 98, 152, 175
Kali 93
Knemu 132
Kundalini 133, 135

L

Limpias 8
Lion 51, 61, 105, 117
Los Angeles 33, 36, 78, 139, 150
Love 4, 7, 12, 38, 52-53, 55, 57, 59, 62-64, 76, 85, 87-90, 95, 99, 101-105, 112, 114, 118, 129, 139, 141-144, 148, 158, 163-164, 167, 175, 187, 190
Lower self 160
Luisa 96-97, 100-103, 105, 108, 118, 149, 161-162, 165, 186, 190

M

Maat 92
Macro-thoughtforms 128, 130
Magic mushrooms 11, 14, 18-19, 147, 154, 156, 157, 158-160, 180, 189
Magician 71-72, 74, 89, 135, 141, 153, 171, 174
Magus ix, 40, 111, 116, 174, 177
Major Arcana 51, 100, 175
Marbella, Spain 135
Maria Elena 91-92
Marques del Valle hotel 7
Master Morya 82, 151
Masters of Shambhala 78
Materias 8

Meditation 5, 7, 53, 69, 70-71, 73, 75, 81, 83-84, 87, 92-93, 96, 101, 113, 147, 149
Melchizedek 57
Mercury 60, 186
Merkabah 71
Merlin 50, 74
Mexicali 79, 96
México City 6, 67, 75, 77, 149, 174
Miahuatlán 10
Mixtec 3, 17, 160

N

Nagual 16, 165-167, 181, 187
Native American 115, 136, 139
Nature x, 3, 6, 12, 15, 42, 51-53, 56, 87-88, 94, 108-109, 112-113, 126, 130, 133, 141, 143-145, 155-156, 160-161, 169, 172, 177-178, 184, 189
Nature spirit 144
Nazi 38, 40, 151
New Age 45, 73, 107, 118, 148, 178
New York City 81
Nu 89

O

Oaxaca 3, 7, 10, 12, 18
Osiris 94, 96-97, 102, 132, 186
Our Lady of Santa Lucia 17

P

Power xi, 4, 9, 12, 36-38, 40, 46-47, 50, 62-63, 77-78, 80-83, 87, 89, 91, 93, 96, 100, 102-103, 105, 110-113, 116-117, 123, 125-126, 135, 137-139, 142-144, 151-152, 156,

158, 160, 162, 164, 166, 177-179, 183
Prince Rackozi 96. *See also* Count St. Germain

Q
Queen of the Wheel of Fortune 16

R
Ramón 33-34, 43-46
Real Self ix, x, 111, 186
Reincarnation 75, 78
Root chakra 144

S
Sai Baba 134
Samadhi 63, 172, 148
San Francisco 55, 70, 134
San José del Pacífico 10, 18, 19
Schwarz, Jack 122
Serpent of Life 6, 118
Setan 176
Seven rays 122
Shakti 100, 148
Sorcerer 14, 16
Sorcery 7, 9, 14, 16, 34, 77, 124
STAR*LIFE (aims, method, and origin) 96, 108-109, 112, 114-118, 136, 138, 166
Starlords 101
Stellar energies 117
Supreme Order of Aquarius 45- 46
Swami Muktananda 135
Synchrony 72, 82, 89, 92, 107, 163, 176, 186
Szandor LaVey, Anton 152

T
Tarot 37, 51, 54, 61, 75, 90, 95, 100, 105, 155, 175, 177. *See also* Major Arcana
Tattwas 115
Tecate 43, 46
Theosophy 78, 113
Thoth 58, 94, 153, 186
Tight-ass syndrome 126
Tijuana 4, 6, 37, 43, 50, 79, 91, 149-150, 175-176
Toltec 160
Transhimalayan Brotherhood 82-83, 96
Transpersonal levels x, 4, 42, 56, 155
Tree of Good and Evil 59-60
Tree of Life 10, 59, 187
Tree of the Universe 59

U
United Nations 81-83, 96-97

V
Vegetarian 33, 150, 168, 171
Venus 59, 87, 89, 99, 100. *See also* Aphrodite
Vesica Pisces 61

W
Warrior 38, 41, 94, 118, 153, 160, 172, 174
Wisdom 5, 10, 18, 54, 57, 59-60, 68, 100, 108, 112-114, 118, 125, 142, 148, 168, 179, 186, 189

Z
Zapotec 160

STAR★LIFE™
INSTANT ACCESS TO COSMIC ENERGIES

With STAR★LIFE you tap directly into the powers of the universe.

The Cosmic Activations given by Luis De La Lama polarize your energy field to receive and radiate specific cosmic energies every time you use simple hand gestures. The first level of STAR★LIFE enables you to apply the powers of the five metaphysical elements to harmonize and fulfill your life as well as that of others.

The STAR★LIFE energies replenish your life force, clear mental, emotional, even physical dysfunctions, and produce spectacular results in self-growth, achievement, and enlightenment. The STAR★LIFE energies are so effective that 96 percent feel their effect right away. They are used professionally by healers, psychologists, chiropractors, massage therapists, counselors, and others in various caretaking roles.

To receive free literature, please call 1-800-441-4111 in the U.S.A. or write to

STAR★LIFE
1295 South Kihei Rd., Suite 3009
Kihei, Maui, HI 96753
U.S.A.

POWER PLANETS
A Manual for Human Empowerment
by Luisa De La Lama

More than just another book on astrology, this is a workbook of meditational exercises and magical practices aimed at revealing the archetypal core of energy at the heart of every planet. The author presents the traditional as well as the more esoteric issues involved in applying astrology's higher principles to personal transcendence and rebirth.

$17.95

Power Planets may be ordered directly from STAR*LIFE. Please add $3 for postage and handling. Prices subject to change without notice.

STAR*LIFE
1295 South Kihei Rd., Suite 3009
Kihei, Maui, HI 96753
U.S.A.

Inner journeys audiotapes to contact the twelve power planets available Spring 1994.

MANIFESTING YOUR SPIRITUAL POWER

Workshop conducted by Luis De La Lama

In Life you either stagnate in a meaningless existence trying to fulfill others' models and expectations, or, finding your core power, you become the creator of an exciting new universe.

You know this experiential weekend is for you when

✔ You want to find out for yourself who you are, where you come from, and where you are going.

✔ You have tried *everything* in the self-help market and still feel your life could be better.

✔ You feel ready to face the chaos masking your true self.

✔ You feel ready to challenge your most basic (and unconscious) assumptions about your parents, God, good and evil, time, and the meaning of life.

✔ You want to assume the responsibility and risk that comes with true power.

For information, please call 1-800-441-4111 in the U.S.A. or write to

STAR*LIFE
1295 South Kihei Rd., Suite 3009
Kihei, Maui, HI 96753
U.S.A.